DISSENT
IN
POLAND

ISBN   0   9506048   0   1

First impression 1977
Second revised impression 1979

DISSENT

IN

POLAND

Reports and Documents
in
Translation

December 1975 — July 1977

Revised second impression

Association of Polish Students
and Graduates in Exile

42 Emperor's Gate, London SW7 4HJ

© 1979

Printed by Veritas Foundation Press, 5 Praed Mews, London W2 1QZ

CONTENTS

———

3

7. PERSPECTIVES FOR THE FUTURE ... 165

FOREWORD

For well over a year now Poland has been seeing the development of a forceful and courageous human rights movement. Its aspirations may be found in the pages of Poland's Constitution; in the Universal Declaration of Human Rights; and in the Final Act signed by the European Heads of State in Helsinki.

The distinguishing feature of this movement is its universality. It has embraced people with widely different traditions and orientations, people of all generations and from diverse groups of society. Its participants include workers and students, priests and scientists, writers and artists, Socialists and Christians. The documents contained in this book bear witness to this movement. They bear witness, also, to Poland's real situation, and to human courage; and, lastly, they testify that the Poles have not accepted their bondage, nor will they ever do so.

Every collectively signed petition to the authorities helps to restore a sense of solidarity and thus puts limits on the oppressiveness of the totalitarian state, an indispensable feature of which is the atomization of society. The documents that follow are thus the true voice of the real Poland, and a record of Poland's consciousness. At the same time, they provide an excellent commentary to the latest events in Poland, which have aroused so much world-wide interest — and understandably so. For if the West European states are reluctant — and, I may say, commendably so — to bring about change in Eastern Europe by the use of military force, then the activity of human rights campaigners is the only source of hope for the evolution of the so-called "socialist state" towards democratic forms of government.

Public opinion in Western Europe and the United States should be informed about Poland's real situation, if only for the reason that it can be influential in changing it. Not infrequently, the actions of people of goodwill and the pressure exerted by them on governments have produced tangible results. Theirs has been one of the most vital roles in protecting

5

those victimized or imprisoned in Eastern Europe. We count on such help from public opinion, and appeal for it to be given.

This collection of documents has been published on the initiative of the Association of Polish Students and Graduates in Exile. This fact provides further testimony, if such be needed, to the solidarity of all Poles, at home and abroad, in striving for the implementation of human rights.

Adam Michnik

PREFACE

The documents which we have assembled in this book unfold the history of a unique and coherent bid to secure fundamental human rights in Poland. They chronicle the attempts of courageous individuals to stand up to the authorities and break the barriers of fear which are a normal feature of everyday life in Poland. In a detailed and systematic way they tell of the anguish and concern felt by the many victims of the system.

The events of 1976 mark a new stage in the evolution of dissent in post-war Poland. Exactly twenty years before, the Stalinist régime had crumbled. It had been a period of mass terror, supervised by Moscow directly, which had even consigned the Primate to imprisonment. The relaxation which came with the new leader, Władysław Gomułka, turned out to be short-lived. Dissent in the early 1960's was limited to localized, occasional, workers' strikes and to a small number of intellectuals and Party members who concerned themselves mostly with censorship and internal reform.

It was not until the student protests of March 1968 that one saw again street demonstrations throughout the country under the banners of democracy and change. These indicated a massive rejection of the system by the generation which had been born and bred in the new Poland. Many student leaders spent some time in jail, but were not deterred from further political activity. Many of them were again to be in the forefront of dissent in 1976. It should be mentioned here that, unlike their Western contemporaries, Polish students in 1968 did not take issue with society but rather stood up in its defence and demanded its fundamental freedoms.

The 1968 protest was exploited by factions within the Party to topple Gomułka. Though the attempt was unsuccessful, the Party leader increasingly became out of touch with the population, as witness the incomprehensible decision to increase food prices by about 25% just before Christmas 1970. The increases provoked riots in the Polish Baltic ports which the police quelled with gunfire. Hundreds of workers were killed. In consequence Gomułka fell from power and the new leader, Edward Gierek, was soon forced by further confronta-

7

tion to rescind the increases. The events of 1970 signalled the rejection now by the workers of the state which is supposedly run by them and for them. However, the workers were alone in their protest; though they looked to the students for support, they were denied it just as they had denied theirs in 1968 to the students.

At the close of 1975 the Party put forward proposals to amend the Constitution. It must seem suprising that this should have sparked off another wave of protest, after all, one might argue that the Constitution was a meaningless document which the Party had never respected. Yet, over 40,000 people, mainly students and intellectuals, of varying political persuasions, signed letters of protest to the Sejm (Polish Parliament). Perhaps it was the myth value of Constitutions in Polish history that moved them. In June 1976 the Party once more attempted a huge increase in food prices without duly preparing and consulting the country. This again provoked the working class to a show of deep indignation in massive demonstrations. By then the various opposition groupings which had become active in the Constitutional issue were ready to co-operate and rally round the workers so that a large concerted front was displayed, stretching through all sections of society: workers, intellectuals and, of course, the Church — that sole bastion of "legalized" opposition which had for long concerned itself with social matters.

This new opposition movement is dedicated, at great personal risk, to the task of bringing about genuine respect for human rights and adherence to the rule of law with the eventual goal of a democratic Poland. In 1968 all the old hopes for reform from within the system had ended, but now a fresh possibility of change by pressures from outside the system had opened. Intellectuals and students took up the cause of the workers bringing financial, legal and medical aid to the victims of repression. They were making a deliberate attempt to break through class barriers. The profound political importance of this lies in the fact that the workers are the only ones who can and have brought down the Communist leadership in Poland.

The opposition movement has been very successful in its short-term objective of securing the release of all the workers who had been imprisoned for their part in the June demonstrations, but it took thousand of petitions, appeals to Western public opinion (amongst others to the Euro-communist leaders), a year's sustained effort and two amnesties. The price paid was harassment and intimidation by Security Service, the frequent 48-hour detentions culminating in the imprisonment of a number of leading dissidents for an unspecified time. The recent second amnesty of 22 July 1977 brought their release (though formally the amnesty could not embrace them). Such was the pressure of public opinion.

The remarkable growth both in numerical terms and political significance of the opposition groupings in Poland is a unique phenomenon for Eastern Europe and a contrasting reality in comparison with the heavily suppressed dissident movements in the USSR and Czechoslovakia. Moreover, the political education which so many people have undergone over the past years will doubtless have crucial consequence for future developments not just in Poland but within the Communist bloc and therefore also in East-West relations.

The translations extracts summaries and accounts were prepared by members of the Association of Polish Students and Graduates in Exile. Their work and this book is dedicated to the many men and women of courage who have suffered in the cause of "bread and freedom".

Executive Committee of the Association of Polish Students and Graduates in Exile

ACKNOWLEDGEMENTS

We wish to thank Mr. G. Schöpflin for his kind comments regarding the preparation of this book.

We are grateful to *Le Monde* for permission to include translations of M. Lucbert's interview with J. Kuroń and also A. Michnik's article "Vive la Pologne!".

9

Chapter one

BEGINNINGS OF CONCERTED DISSENT: OPPOSITION TO CHANGES IN THE CONSTITUTION

On 10th February 1976 the Polish Sejm (Parliament) ratified the New Constitution of the Polish People's Republic, replacing that of 22nd July 1952. Despite an avalanche of objections, protests and petitions from intellectuals, artists, Church dignitaries and the general public not a single member of the Sejm voted against the proposals, and only one — Dr. W. Stomma — abstained.

THE PROPOSED AMENDMENTS

Plans to revise the Constitution had been mooted as early as the VI Party Congress in December 1971, but only in very general terms. A more specific declaration of intent was made by Party First Secretary Edward Gierek in his speech to the Sejm in July 1974, on the occasion of the 30th Anniversary of People's Poland. "We should", he said, "form the Constitution of our State in such a way as to make it an even stronger foundation on which to construct a developed socialist society and to implement fully the principles of socialism in all areas of the nation's life." Further details were given in the Agenda and Guidelines for the VII Party Congress in the second half of 1975, which included the following passage:

"In particular, the historic fact that the Polish People's Republic is a socialist state in which the power belongs to the working people of the towns and villages and the leading force is the Polish United Workers' Party, must be confirmed in the Constitution."

A second key proposal was announced on 19th December 1975 by Party official Edward Babiuch, who told the Sejm that "confirmed in the Constitution should be the principle of Poland's foreign policy, its participation in the world socialist system, its unshakeable fraternal bond with the Soviet Union."

Together, these two proposed amendments, or additions, were designed to bring Poland into line with the other East European countries, all of whose Constitutions have references to a "socialist state" and (with the notable exception of Romania) to links with the Soviet Union. If introduced, they would legalise the two-fold non-sovereignty of Poland: the non-sovereignty of its government, which is neither freely elected, nor responsible to, the people; and the non-sovereignty of the state in its dependence on a foreign power. The legalization of the latter would ultimately be the more significant: a friendship or alliance implies *that either side can speak out, and act, if it considers that its partner is not fulfilling his obligations; and an assurance of friendship, would, if it found its way into Poland's fundamental statute, offer the Soviet leaders great scope for interpretation.*

A further proposed amendment gave cause for concern, viz. that "citizens' rights are inseparably linked with honest fulfilment of their duties towards their motherland". Again, this would allow room for interpretation; it could be used as an excuse for depriving those who were critical or unorthodox in their views, of civil rights and liberties.

OPPOSITION TO THE PARTY'S PROPOSALS

Despite the possibility of repression, a wide cross-section of the Polish community openly expressed its opposition to the proposed changes. This was done principally through open letters, petitions and statements signed by individuals, or groups of individuals, and addressed to the authorities — a form of protest by no means unprecedented. In 1964 34 prominent intellectuals had submitted an open letter protesting against censorship; in 1968 there were signed protests against the banning of one of Poland's major plays, Forefathers' Eve, *from the stage of the National Theatre in Warsaw; numerous other petitions were submitted on various occasions. Never before, however, had such large numbers appealed to the authorities on one issue. Surprisingly, even for the signatories themselves, an opposition movement emerged and made itself known, just as it was to do in Czechoslovakia over* Charter 77, *approximately a year later; socialists, Christians, ex-Marxists joined forces in defending, if only on paper, the sovereignty of their country.*

The Manifesto of the 59

On 5th December 1975 the Speaker of the Sejm received an open letter signed by 59 of Poland's most prominent intellectuals, artists, writers and scientists. It was this manifesto that launched the wave of protests, though it did not take issue with any particular proposals, having been prepared before the VII Party Congress; rather, it demanded that the fundamental rights and liberties already guaranteed in the Constitution be implemented in practice.

"The directives for the VII Party Congress of the PZPR (Polish United Workers' Party)" include the announcement of a change in the Constitution. Following the conference in Helsinki, during which the Polish government, together with the governments of 34 other nations, formally asserted the Universal Declaration of Human Rights, we consider that the introduction of these basic freedoms should constitute a new milestone in the history of our country and in the life of individuals. Prompted by our civic concern, we feel that the

12

Constitution and the legislation based on it should above all guarantee the following civil rights:

— Freedom of conscience and religious practice. These freedoms do not exist when people professing religious beliefs or expressing an ideology other than that which is officially made compulsory are barred from a considerable number of key posts in public offices and institutions, in social organizations and in the national economy. Therefore all citizens, irrespective of their religion, ideology or party-political affiliation, must be assured of an equal right to take up government posts. The deciding factors for such appointments should only be one's qualifications, ability and personal integrity. The free practice of religion and the building of places of worship must also be made possible for all denominational groups.

— Freedom of work. There is no such freedom while the State is the sole employer, and while Trade Unions are forced to conform to the administration of the Party, which actually wields the power in the State. In conditions such as these — as the events of 1956 and 1970 testify — any attempts to protect the workers' interests are threatened by bloodshed and can lead to serious outbreaks of violence. For this reason employees must be assured their freedom to choose their own trade representation, which is independent of both State and Party. The right to strike must also be guaranteed.

— Freedom of speech and exchange of information. When there is no freedom of speech, national culture cannot develop freely. When all publications are submitted to State censorship before appearing in print, and when the publication and the mass media are State-controlled, the citizens cannot consciously develop an attitude towards decisions taken by the State authorities, while at the same time the State is unaware of the public's attitude to its policy. Some particularly grave consequences of the State's monopoly over publications and the workings of preventive censorship can be seen in literature and art, which do not fulfil their socially significant functions. It must therefore be made possible for the Trade Unions and for the creative, religious and other societies to bring out books and periodicals without State intervention. Preventive censorship must therefore be abolished, while in the event of an infringement of the publishing statute, the law should be enforced only by means of legal proceedings.

13

— Freedom in education. There can be no freedom in education as long as the criteria for the selection of teaching staff and subjects for study are determined by State authority, and as long as these criteria are of a political nature. Therefore the academic freedom of the establishments of higher education must be brought back, and the academic circles must not be denied their right to autonomy.

It is impossible for the assurance of these basic freedoms to be reconciled with the recent officially-prepared declaration regarding the leading role of one of the parties in the system of State authority. A constitutional assertion of this type would give to the political party the role of an instrument of State authority, not responsible to nor controlled by the public. Under such conditions Parliament cannot be regarded as the highest instrument of authority, the Government is not the highest executive body, and the courts are not independent.

All citizens must be assured that they will achieve their right to nominate and vote for their representatives according to the accepted democratic principles of free elections. The courts must be assured of their independence from the executive power, and the highest legislative power must effectively be given to Parliament. We believe that the disregard of civil rights may lead to the destruction of general resourcefulness, to the dissolution of social bonds, to a gradual loss of national identity, and finally to a discontinuation of national tradition. Indeed, it constitutes a threat to the nation's very existence.

The assertions and postulates which we are submitting express the conviction that the responsibility for the destiny of our society is shared by all.

The recognition of these freedoms, confirmed at the Helsinki Conference, has today assumed international importance, for where there is no freedom, there can neither be peace nor security.

Stefan Amsterdamski, Stanisław Barańczak, Ewa Bieńkowska, Jacek Bierezin, Irena Byrska, Tadeusz Byrski, Bohdan Chwedeńczuk, Ludwik Cohn, Andrzej Drawicz, Jerzy Ficowski, Kornel Filipowicz, Zbigniew Herbert, Ryszard Herczyński, Maryla Hopfinger, Zdzisław Jaroszewski, Anna Kamieńska, Jakub Karpiński, Wojciech Karpiński, Jan Kielanowski, Stefan Kisielewski, Jacek Kleyff, Leszek Kołakowski, Julian Kornhauser, Maria Korniłowicz, Marcin Król, Ryszard Krynicki, Jacek Ku-

roń, Stanisław Leśniewski, Edward Lipiński, Jan Józef Lipski, Zdzisław Łapiński, Rev. Stanisław Małkowski, Jerzy Markuszewski, Adam Mauersberger, Adam Michnik, Halina Mikołajska, Jan Nepomucen Miller, Ludwik Muzyczka, Zygmunt Mycielski, Jerzy Narbutt, Jan Olszewski, Antoni Pajdak, Krzysztof Pomian, Józef Rybicki, Rev. Jacek Salij, Władysław Siła-Nowicki, Stanisław Skalski, Antoni Słonimski, Aniela Steinsbergowa, Julian Stryjkowski, Jan Józef Szczepański, Adam Szczypiorski, Kazimierz Szelągowski, Wisława Szymborska, Jacek Trznadel, Maria Wosiek, Adam Zagajewski, Wacław Zawadzki, Rev. Jan Zieja.

FURTHER PROTESTS

Further open letters followed immediately; submitting the Manifesto of the 59, Professor Edward Lipiński advised the Speaker of the Sejm that a memorandum signed by over 300 students, scholars and lecturers would follow shortly. Former Minister W. Bieńkowski sent a letter to the Party daily newspaper, Trybuna Ludu, which, not surprisingly, did not publish it. A protest and demand for a referendum on the subject was submitted by a group of 20 people from Łódź, including manual workers, lawyers and a priest; other memoranda were sent by representatives of the "Catholic Intelligentsia Clubs" and editors of Catholic publications. The Letter of the 14, dealing with the "fraternal bond with the Soviet Union", and the Memorandum of 101, which discusses the rights and duties of the citizen, are two documents which epitomize the principal anxieties and demands voiced by the public over the issue of the Constitution.

Letter of the 14

At a session of Parliament on January 9th Edward Babiuch, speaking on behalf of the Parliamentary Polish United Workers' Party, declared that "Constitutional confirmation should be made of the principles governing Polish foreign policy: membership of the world socialist system and the inviolable fraternal bond with the Soviet Union...".

The lawfulness of the treaty obligations of the Polish People's Republic is beyond doubt. But incorporating the provisions of a treaty of alliance into the Statutes of the Constitution and raising them to the rank of a fundamental constitutional principle is universally acknowledged as a limitation of a country's sovereignty.

15

Modern International Law considers the essence of sovereignty to lie in the equality of rights and obligations of nations. This principle has guided the community of nations in the last thirty post-war years to recognize the complete independence of a number of colonial and semi-dependent countries. It has recently also found full confirmation in the text of the Helsinki Agreement.

The proposed changes to the Constitution are in blatant contradiction to this current of our times. A unilaterally established constitutional principle providing for the inviolability of an alliance with a neighbouring state, in the form of a binding internal statute, would reduce the Polish People's Republic to the status of formally limited sovereignty. Enactment of this anachronistic notion of political law would threaten our country with degradation of its political significance.

Ever since the Great French Revolution, the principle of national sovereignty has been an unquestioned asset of progressive political thought. It was the guiding light in our country's struggle for national independence and also for the inseparably connected social emancipation of the Polish people; it was at the heart of the reborn Polish State and found expression in the [new] Republic's first Constitution of 17 March 1921. It is respected by art. 1 of the Constitution of the Polish People's Republic as at present in force.

In this historical, constitutional tradition there is no place for a principle legally providing for the leading role of another country or for unilateral renouncement of the prerogatives of sovereign foreign policy. For such must be the interpretation of the recognition of an international alliance as a constitutional norm binding only one of its signatories.

The inviolate principle of a nation's sovereignty does not authorize any whatsoever of its representatives to legislate contrary to this principle.

The tragic experiences of our national history, from the Dumb Parliament of 1717, through one partition after another, right until the final collapse of statehood, do not allow us Poles to forget the precepts of history. They force us to remember that each agreement to accept unilateral constitutional guarantees or unilateral guarantes of alliance from a neighbouring power was a first step to the obliteration of Poland's name from the political map of Europe.

16

The boundless degradation and sufferings which followed such events have stamped an indelible mark on the nation's national security. Treaty obligations of over thirty years standing between Poland and the USSR have forged a new historical relationship between our nations. It is for this reason that the proposed constitutional changes are superfluous.

Stefan Amsterdamski, Władysław Bartoszewski, Ludwik Cohn, Jerzy Ficowski, Maria Hopfinger, Jacek Kuroń, Edward Lipiński, Jan Józef Lipski, Zdzisław Łapiński, Adam Michnik, Zbigniew Raszewski, Antoni Słonimski, Aniela Steinsbergowa, Jacek Trznadel.

Memorandum of the 101

Notices published some time ago [of amendments to the present Constitution of the Polish People's Republic] have awakened anxieties, to which public opinion has given expression amongst others in collective and individual letters. Now that PAP [Polish Press Agency] has released information regarding the recently prepared proposals of changes to the Constitution, the anxieties of the public must, unfortunately, be regarded as well founded. In associating ourselves with the anxieties and protests voiced earlier, we, the undersigned, consider as particularly dangerous to society the proposal to add to art. 57 the assertion: "The rights of citizens are inseparably connected with an honest and conscientious fulfilment of obligations to the motherland".

Democracy in general, and hence too socialist democracy, assumes that enjoyment of civil rights cannot be limited by any special conditions, let alone conditions whose formulation is unclear and allows arbitrary interpretation by government offices and individuals mandated with authority. For example, persons, whose political views differ from those of the Party, the Party being described in a later passage of the proposals as "the leading force of society", would be denied civil rights, as would also persons adopting a critical attitude to the current methods of government. It is well known that even persons convicted to imprisonment for definite criminal offences may not be deprived of civil rights except by a separate lawful ruling of the court. If another article of the present Constitution assures citizens of "freedom of speech, publication, assembly, mass meetings, marches and demonstrations" then further articles cannot be introduced which would hold the enjoyment of these particular freedoms as contrary in certain circumstances to "honest and conscientious fulfilment of obligations to the motherland" and in consequence deny the right to enjoy these freedoms. In a situation where limitations of the above freedoms in the Polish People's Republic are actually visible and continually progressing (increasing pressure of censorship contrary to the freedom of speech and publication) the introduction of the cited addition to art. 57 would have to be interpreted unambiguously as a serious and even decisive step in the direction of legalizing total control of all aspects of life in our country and endangering fundamental civil rights and freedoms.

A Comment on the Consultative Procedure

Among the letters on the subject of constitutional amendments was one signed by 92 students from universities in Warsaw, Lublin and on the Coast.

Dear Mr. Speaker,

We wish to place in your hands our protest against the way in which the amendments to the Constitution of the Polish People's Republic were passed. Such an important area of legislation as amendment of the fundamental statute is a matter for the whole nation and should be put to an all-national discussion. However our society did not have the opportunity to acquaint itself with the proposed changes until January 26th, whereas by February 10th Parliament had already approved the amendments. Thus, 15 days separated the publication date of the proposals from the moment of their approval — too short a time interval for everyone to voice their opinion. For it is a misunderstanding to claim that the issue had been under discussion for four years. No person unconnected with central Government or Party agencies could form an opinion until after the publication of a general outline of the changes, i.e. not until after January 26th. In any case the proposals were nowhere published in full, but only in fragmentary form. The pretence of a discussion that was staged in the mass media was too one-sided to permit Members of Parliament to make themselves familiar with the public's attitude. And throughout the discussion, publication of critical views was not allowed.

The amendment of the Constitution has resulted in a number of changes that give cause for concern, namely:

1) The institutionalization of the PZPR [Polish United Workers' Party] as the leading political force, a fact that has nothing to do with democracy, even with socialist democracy. The PZPR is according to its own constitution an atheist party, so that its institutionalization places in jeopardy religious freedom and de facto quashes the equality of right of believers.

2) The unilateral constitutional guarantees of ties with a neighbouring state which lead to a limitation of our sovereignty.

The attitude of the Polish Catholic Church

The position of the Church was made clear in the sternly worded sermons given by Cardinal Stefan Wyszyński, the Primate of Poland, and by Cardinal Wojtyła. An official statement regarding the Church's position was issued on 9th January 1976, following a conference of the Hierarchy, and updated by an additional statement issued on 26th January 1976.

A much fuller exposé of the Church's attitude to the Constitutional changes was made public in a pastoral letter read from church pulpits in April i.e., after the new Constitution was put into effect. This document is reproduced in full on page 20.

Final Outcome: a minor climb-down

The repercussions of the protests will be felt in Poland for a long time to come, because of the strong unity and solidarity established over the constitutional issue; but the pressure applied on the authorities achieved some immediate results as well, in that the phrasing of each of the controversial articles of the Constitution was toned down. The vow of an "inviolable fraternal bond" with the Soviet Union was amended to a statement that the Polish People's Republic "strengthens its friendship and co-operation with the USSR and other socialist countries". The Party's role, which was to have been written in as that of "the leading politcal force" was reduced to the less autocratic "guiding political force in the construction of socialism". On citizens' duties, the final version states that "the citizens of the Polish People's Republic should honestly fulfil their duties towards the motherland and contribute to its development", but does not make civil rights a privilege dependent on such conduct.

An appraisal of the constitutional debate

Explanatory Statement by the Secretariate of the Polish Hierarchy
Regarding the Proposed Changes to the Constitution

The Catholic community in Poland is interested in the position taken by the Episcopate with regard to the proposed changes to the Constitution of the Polish People's Republic. A short communiqué on the matter was issued for the information of the faithful on February 18th, immediately after the 151st Episcopal Conference. The faithful are making numerous enquiries about the Church and the rights of believers under the new scheme. In order to give a reply, if only in part, the following somewhat fuller explanation is offered.

I. The Bishops lodged two Memoranda with the relevant authorities. These were dated 9th January and 26th January and expounded the basic demands of the Catholic community necessary for maintaining harmony, peace of life and coexistence in our common motherland.

The Constitution is the fundamental statute by means of which the sovereign Nation has the right and duty to safeguard the basic rights of its citizens and to define its system of government. The Episcopate considered it their duty to express their views as the greater part of the community, who are subject to the provisions of the Constitution, are members of the Catholic Church. The issue was not only of a government nature but also a moral and social one. The Bishops, as representatives of the Church and as citizens of their country, have an absolute right and duty to express themselves on this matter.

As is known from official statements, the proposed changes to the Constitution called forth a number of declarations and documents addressed to the Commission on the Constitution. These were lodged by legal means. Their authors and signatories wished to fulfil their civil obligations and expressed their concern for the common good. All this testifies to the sensibilities of a society which possesses a historical consciousness gained through the experience of history over the centuries. Without doubt this society is particularly sensitive to the indispensable rights of man and to the indispensable rights of the Nation. In so far as human rights are concerned, our society understands them in the spirit of its national tradition of respect for the freedom of the individual and for

20

Declaration of Human Rights, reaffirmed at the Conference in Helsinki. The documents of the Vatican Council refer to these same rights as do the encyclicals of John XXIII and Paul VI (in particular "Pacem in terris" and „Populorum progressio").

With regard to the rights of the Nation, it must be remembered that they were bought at the cost of a century's toil and struggle in the cultural field and on the battle-field — to mention only the last world war — and with many other sacrifices. We therefore set a singularly high value on them.

II. The following are the basic themes of the Episcopate's statement to the Parliamentary Commission in the above-mentioned Memoranda.

1. The Bishops expressed anxieties arising from the intention to confirm in the Constitution the Party's leading role in the State. They drew attention to the danger resulting from this of a division of citizens into two categories and of subjecting the whole of our life to the materialist outlook which would be unacceptable to believers.

2. The Bishops expressed anxieties arising from the intention to confirm in the Constitution Poland's membership of the world socialist system. They drew attention to the fact that the Constitution may not contain anything that would limit the sovereignty of the Nation and of the Polish State. The Episcopate recalled principles such as sovereign equality, inviolable frontiers, non-interference in internal affairs etc. which were accepted at Helsinki.

3. The Bishops expressed concern that the freedom of citizens' rights and responsibilities should not be limited by a single ideological outlook and philosophical system.

III. With reference to these widely felt anxieties, the following demands were made.

1. The State has a duty to respect and safeguard the rights of every Person-Man-Citizen. Indispensable civil rights may not be conditional on the fulfilment of duties.

2. The State has a duty to respect the rights of the family and to aid it in the fulfillment of its parental obligations. Particular prominence was given to the priority of the family over the professions and other social and political groups.

3. The Constitution should safeguard those favourable conditions needed for the Nation's development consistent with its history, culture and merits. The Nation cannot be absorbed into any supranational or suprastate body.

4. The Church, conjoined with the Nation by a common history, has through its service and its deserving historic contributions a right to due respect for its mission. Freedom of the Church and the individual's freedom of conscience and of religious practice both public and private are the requisites for social harmony in the life of the Nation and of the State.

5. The Constitution should guarantee that the State be able to carry out its duties by means of the appropriate institutions of Parliament, Government, independent judicial system and civil service, free trade unions. The Government must be aware of its obligations to all sections of the Nation and fulfil them equitably and without hindrance. Parliament should be assembled by free elections and should be the guardian of all civil rights and duties.

6. The Episcopate's Memorandum recalled the social and economic rights of the farming population and i.a. those of the private farmers who constitute an important section of society from the point of view of land cultivation and the provision of food.

7. The right of the Nation and of the State to preserve complete sovereignty in the domains of national culture, economic freedom and of its own aims should be emphasized and guaranteed by the Constitution. It is in order to recall here the rights of nations to self-determination as described in the UN Charter and as reaffirmed at the Conference in Helsinki.

IV. Further to the above explanatory remarks, it should be noted that over the last few years, since 1970, the Episcopate has submitted a number of documents to the State Authorities on such subjects as the basic rights of the Church, the Catholic community, believers, and the normalizations of relations between State and Church. In view of their contents, these too were of paramount importance to the future Constitution. The Bishops drew attention to matters of vital social importance, such as: biological dangers, defence of life, respect for religious freedom, rights of Christian culture, imperilment of the freedom of conscience of the young, the work-code, equal rights of promotion in the professions, the constitutional principle of civil equality, etc.

At the present moment, albeit after the approval of the Constitution by Parliament, all the issues which were raised in earlier and in recent memoranda continue to be as relevant as before. The communiqué of the 151st Episcopal Conference states that, although the Authorities have partly taken into consideration demands made by the Episcopate and by citizens from various sections of society, there nevertheless remain demands which were not met, but which are a source of particular anxiety to public opinion, to the Church and to believers.

The Episcopate therefore have not ceased their appeals to the Authorities on whom also rests responsibility for the future of the Nation and for the equitable treatment of all citizens. The issue is of acute interest not only to Poles in Poland but also to the multitude of Polish emigrés throughout the world who share in common with us the joys and tribulations of their country.

We all expect that those who responded to the appeals of the Extraordinary Commission on the Constitution and made their views known by legal means in documents sent to the Commission, will be respected. They availed themselves of rights which were due to them as free citizens. They fulfilled their moral and political duties and in so doing proved their civil maturity. Respect for the inviolable rights of man, of his person, is the fundamental task of a just social system and state. Such respect goes hand in hand with respect for the rights of the Polish Nation, a nation that after historic experiences and endeavours deserves a sovereign existence as a state of its own.

Warsaw, dated March 1976.

On the instructions of the Principal Council of the Polish Episcopate,

Bishop Br. Dąbrowski
Secretary to the Episcopate.

Reprisals by the Authorities

The reprisal most frequently employed against signatories of the letters of protest (as a punitive measure, and deterrent for the future) was the refusal of a passport for a journey abroad; but harsher action was taken against some of the more prominent signatories. Producer and director Jerzy Markuszewski was dismissed from his post with Polish Radio (the cast he was directing in a series of satirical programmes resigned as a gesture of solidarity). The popular songwriter and singer Wojciech Młynarski was until recently banned from performing, and the performance of his songs and their broadcast on radio were not permitted. A number of writers and critics had books withdrawn from publication, or articles rejected by periodicals, ostensibly on grounds of merit or lack of space. An indication of the pettiness of some of the measures may be given by the fact that an entire issue of the weekly Ekran *("Screen") was withdrawn from circulation because its cover carried a large photograph of Aleksandra Śląska, actress and a signatory of the letter of 101.*

Chapter two

CRITIQUE BY TWO EMINENT SOCIALISTS

Professor EDWARD LIPIŃSKI, born 1888, is one of the foremost of Polish economists. He was Professor at the Central School of Planning and Statistics and at the University of Warsaw and is a member of the Polish Academy of Sciences. He was vice-chairman of the Economic Council in the years 1956-62, president of the Economists' Association from 1946 to 1965 and editor-in-chief of the Polish journal "The Economist". Before the last war he belonged to the Polish Socialist Party and was founder and director of the Institute for Market and Price Research. After the war he turned his attention to the history of political and economic thought and to the theory of socialist political economy.

Professor Lipiński has always played a very prominent role in the Polish dissident movement and has remained boldly outspoken despite many distasteful reprisals. He is well remembered in the West for his part in the protest against censorship in 1964 as signatory of the "letter of 34 intellectuals" and as signatory of the "letter of the 59" (p. 12) against the changes to the Polish Constitution. He takes up this last theme in the Open Letter which follows.

OPEN LETTER TO COMRADE EDWARD GIEREK

Dear Comrade First Secretary,

I am taking the liberty of troubling you with yet another letter, even though there have undoubtedly been too many of them recently. On one occasion my concern was an appeal to free political prisoners who were serving long sentences by reason of an unjust verdict, on another the granting of the right of amnesty to some young people who were refused this right by an unlawful court ruling, and then again there was a letter on the subject of the principles according to which justice should be administered and on the sad state of prisons in our country or again there was a question of the distinguished Society for the Protection of Animals which is being heartlessly destroyed by bureaucracy. Another letter related to the arrest of some very young people for alleged political offences. Together with other representatives of the Polish intelligentsia I demanded proper treatment of the Polish minority in the USSR.

On various occasions and many times I petitioned that employment appropriate to qualifications be given to the research scientists who were deprived of their posts following the organised campaign of reprisals and the administrative decisions of March 1968.

It is with great regret that I must observe that each of my representations on these quite definite issues was not only more and more unsuccessful, but evoked an increasingly unfavourable response from the authorities. Yet not so long ago I was made Honoured Teacher of the Polish People's Republic, and earlier I was accorded for my research and teaching work the Order of the Banner of Labour — First Class — and was made Commander of the Order of the Rebirth of Poland. I was given the National Prize of First Order. As a result of my representations, I have now been subjected to various reprisals. This leads me to conclude that as a socialist there is only one way for me to act so as to be socially useful: by carrying out a critique of the groundwork upon which such and similar phenomena may appear.

In a letter to the delegates of the VII Congress lodged with you on 6th December last, I demanded together with other signatories the basic reform of government and party administration which had been promised just after the tragic events of December 1970 on the Coast, but never implemented, and which were to remove the shortcomings that had led to these events. Thereafter I tried to take part in the officially announced public discussion of changes to the Fundamental Statute. I have reason to suppose that very many of our citizens objected in collective and individual letters against the proposed changes put forward by the governing leadership. Moreover I know for a fact that most of the letters supporting the proposed changes were written on official instructions by employees of government institutions according to a centrally devised register. The public character of the debate on the constitution amounted to this, that the mass media published exclusively those voicing approval. In accord with a thus fabricated national will, our Parliament almost unanimously approved the changes to the Constitution with some minor concessions to public opinion. Dead silence surrounded the protests and voices of criticism. One could therefore feel gratified to hear that at a recent press meeting, you briefly dealt with these voices of public opinion. You discussed the protests and voices of criticism. One could therefore feel "letter of the 59" referring to it no doubt by synecdoche as the "... letter sent by Professor Lipiński". But unfortunately what you said on the subject bears no relation to the contents of the letter, whilst your method of criticism reminds one of the worst times when criticism was dealt with by recourse to epithets and incantations.

Our letter demanded that fundamental freedoms and civil rights be honoured and guaranteed: the freedom of conscience and religious practice, the freedom of work, the freedom of speech and of information and the freedom of science and education. Thus it proposed problems whose solution is of like interest to all representatives of democratic public opinion whether of socialist or Christian leanings.

You considered that our letter questioned "clauses concerned with the role of the Party in the life of the country and the principles of our foreign policy" and then you commented: "... what is this Comrades? This is a feeble attempt at resuscitating the theories of the Polish bourgeois camp which have been compromised by history — theories which led to military defeat in September 1939 and the tragic consequent subjection. It is an attempt to apply notions that have long outserved their use, to a new epoch. Those who have undertaken this attempt, have not understood anything nor learned anything in these last thirty years. They are blind to the obvious fact that relying on the only certain principle of alliance with the Soviet Union, our nation has for already thirty-one years lived in peace, that for the first time in history she has allies for neighbours, that her frontiers are universally recognised, that she has a reliable guarantee of independent existence and finally that co-operation with socialist brother countries is a powerful lever in the development of our economy. It is anticommunist pig-headedness, it is political blindness that prevent them from understanding the national interest."

These are strong words. I am trying to understand what political reasons dictated them. In the letter of the 59 we wrote nothing at all about foreign policy or alliances. If despite this the letter has been criticized from this point of view, I suppose the reasoning behind this is the following. Alliance with the Soviet Union, co-operation with the Socialist countries have

27

assured peace, safe frontiers, and provided a lever in the development of our economy. Hence this alliance and this co-operation are over-riding matters as far as our national existence and safety are concerned. So for the sake of over-riding matters we must act in the same way as our neighbours and allies. Our home policies, our social and political life, the range of civil rights, our cultural life must be approximately such as not to hinder our co-operation with our neighbours, mainly the Soviet Union.

Respected Comrade Secretary, you hold in our system of government an office which is far too prominent for such political appraisals to be passed over without comment. Since, unfortunately, I read the lessons which Poles and all who are involved in socialism should glean from the history of our three decades quite differently to you, I feel obliged to give public expression to my views on the matters which you raised. As one who has been connected for 70 years with the Socialist movement, I feel responsible for the political practice which is advertised in my country as socialism.

As a measure of the successes of the past thirty years of government, the Polish United Workers' Party proclaimed at its last Congress a slogan which has been written into the Constitution: that we live in a socialist society. Nevertheless not even the most beautiful of words can give birth to new socialist inter-human relations, nor to a new, more creative characteristic of human work, nor to equality of men, nor to partnership between superiors and their subordinates, between citizens and their authorities. There is still no theory which would scientifically analyse the means whereby a socialist society may be attained after nationalization of production. I have for a long time been studying the development of socialist thought in the West, particularly in Italy (since such thought has completely stagnated here and in the Soviet Union). I am taking note of recent events in France and Portugal, I am carefully studying the development of political practice in the USSR and I am coming to the conclusion that the Soviet way, which is founded on a tradition of despotic Russian governance, and which is hampering the present development of the Soviet Union, is not a way along which Socialist practice should move in Poland.

From the beginning, Poland would have developed differently had it not been for the pressures that the USSR had

brought to bear. There would have been no forced collectivization, the six-year plan would have been carried out in its
original form. Later, if our Party had consistently followed the
path of November 1956, Poland would have been today an
incomparably more developed country, economically, socially
and morally. Unfortunately this is not the path we took. We
continue to hold fast to the Soviet political system for the sake
of consolidating power and no doubt — above all — under the
pressures of the Soviet Union. There is accordingly, no matter
more important for Poland than gaining political sovereignty.
Only political independence will allow consistent economic
reform, a reconstruction of the political and social system that
would liberate the country's potential creative forces, by elim-
inating the numberless obstacles and constraints which hinder
social development today. This would enable a fundamental
reform in the educational system, improve conditions of research, open the way to full information on home and foreign
affairs, heal internal political relations, put an end to the chaos
resulting from the double administration of Party and State.

Nobody doubts that an alliance with the Soviet Union has
become a political necessity. We hold in esteem the great Soviet
nation, the brother nations of the Ukraine and Byelorussia.
We desire good-neighbourly relations, we wish to lay foundations of mutual confidence. But this will not be possible until
Polish policies with regard to the Soviet Union are radically
cleared of all elements of subservience. This will also not be
possible until the Soviet Union boldly and openly confesses
to "errors" committed against Poland. It is not with the intention of stirring up bitter feelings that I return to this painful
matter. To impose upon us in these circumstances a love towards the Soviet state and to introduce it into the Fundamental
Statute, is to base oneself on complete ignorance of human
psychology. Every Pole remembers only too well the "diabolic"
Ribbentrop–Molotov pact, the invasion of our country, the
mass deportations to prison camps in 1944 and 1945 of soldiers
of the anti-Hitler underground army, and of the Polish intelligentsia who actively engaged against the Germans, and the
absence of help during the Warsaw uprising... I repeat once
more: all this could be forgotten, if the government of the
Soviet Union openly denounced these crimes. Khruschev made
a step in this direction. Inequality in trade deals (coal) was
acknowledged, the dissolution in 1938 of the Polish Communist

Party was denounced and some of its murdered leaders rehabilitated. The "Polish road to Socialism" was briefly accepted. But that is where it ended, and even the German pact is still evasively defended.

Poland has a rich tradition of parliamentarianism, of civil liberties and tolerance. The traditions of a total or police state are alien to us. The imposition of the Soviet system has wrought much havoc in our social and moral life. It was a great calamity in the history of our nation. We are forced to support unconditionally Soviet foreign policy, we have ceased to be an independent factor in world politics. This is often contrary to Polish national interests. We played an active part in the military invasion of Czechoslovakia, we helped to suppress a process of renovation in that country just as it was freeing itself from an imposed Soviet system of economic and cultural policy which checked the country's development. The Czech and Slovak nations will hold this against us for a long time. We violated their sovereignty for the sake of the Soviet Union's imperialist interests and thereby made our own dependence more permanent. In the United Nations Organisation we always vote with the Soviet Union, supporting even the most backward motions — for example the recent recognition of Zionism as racism.

In the whole world, even among Communists, negative attitudes towards the Soviet Union's politics are gaining strength. Understanding for political democracy in its age-old sense is increasing, the slogans of a proletarian or of a one-party dictatorship are being abandoned. This stems not only, as is indeed sometimes the case, from political tactics, but also from the recognition of the essence of the social process, the process of formation of a socialist society, and from a growing understanding of the negative aspects of the Soviet system.

The world communist movement is entering a new period of development. This is also the response to the half-century-old experiment of the Soviet Union, to Stalinism, to military intervention in Hungary and Czechoslovakia, to the process of denunciation connected with the works of Solzhenitsyn, to the enterprise of the great scientist Sakharov.

In the Latin countries the communist movement is a great political force and the moment is not far off when Italian and French communists will actively take part in the governing of their countries. But at the same time communism in Italy,.

France, Spain and elsewhere has undergone deep changes. The movement propagates political pluralism in place of the mono-party system, proclaims the necessity to maintain all the democratic liberties, for which mankind has fought for centuries, free elections, full freedom of the word, the decisive role of a majority in society. These parties have forgone their function of agents of the imperialist interests of the Soviet Union, they wish to determine their own policies, national policies. These changes and ideological transformations are of great historical significance. They are an important step on the road to authentic socialism.

The road is long, difficult and arduous. For socialism is not the child of ideology, that is of faith, but may only be the outcome of changes in the organization of production (the replacement of conveyor belts by a system of small workshops in the Volvo plant in Kalmar is of greater significance to the formation of socialism than the nationalization of the plant) via the transformation of hierarchical, social and political structures into structures of partnership and dialogue, via realization in deeds not just in words, of communal decision-making by the society in its own affairs, via general welfare, and also via the growth of the creative element in work and of beauty in everyday life.

Socialism is an economic system in which production serves to satisfy needs and industries are valued from the point of view of such aims. Needs are just such as production can satisfy and such as is the state of culture and education of the human mass. Consumption is the production of qualities of life and consumption is just such as production. Needs may be shaped, educated, directed. Capitalism manipulates needs by advertising and offering definite goods, for example cars which are available to all. Cars then determine the main core of a country's production, the style of mass consumption, and even the appearance of cities and landscapes.

Consumption patterns may be shaped by educating the masses, by bringing them closer to the treasures of culture, by extending access to the dimension of beauty, by exerting an influence on the human environment in the home, in the housing estate, in the landscape, in the factory, in the office. If at the same time production technology is changed, we may give new shape to work, we may increase human creativity by humanizing the process of production itself. All this could amount to planning consumption and planning a new higher quality of life or rather the possibility of attaining quality in life, since, on last analysis, man himself is the only one who can give value to his life. Economic welfare cannot by itself give to life its meaning, as may easily be seen by looking at countries which have a high welfare. Socialism is an attempt to create the objective conditions which will enable men to find these values.

I have learned much in the course of the last thirty years. I know today better than ever that socialism is not tantamount to the complete bureaucratization of the economy and of public administration nor to the imposition of the so-called materialist world outlook, nor to compulsory atheism. The basis of socialism is freedom, decentralization, co-responsibility of citizens in the decision-making of economic, political and social affairs. It is for this reason that we should demand a democratic system to replace the Soviet system which threatens the process of development of the Nation's energies. It is true that the world is now faced with a crisis in traditional parliamentary democracy. It is equally true that our experiences with democracy in Poland in the interwar years were none too good. Indeed they were very bad. But that is not a reason for accepting the view that Poland's pre-war politics led to "military defeat in September 1939 and consequent subjection". That is too simplified a view to be agreed with. For even communist rule in Poland at the time would not have averted Hitler's attack. When war broke out, any Poland would have had to lose, and would have had to suffer subjection for as long as she in fact did.

And is the monoparty better? I remember the times of Bierut. Mistakes were made and even crimes committed. Tens of thousands were thrown into prison for long years, were subjected to sophisticated torture. We remember the insane programme of collectivization of farms and the ruining of agriculture, thoughtless destruction of the crafts. The bloody riots in Poznań put an end to the system. The Gomułka era ended in upheaval on the Coast and the shameless smothering of worker demonstrations. A political system is not efficient if it is deprived of mechanisms of continual adaptation, if it is rigid, if it destroys critical opinion, if it is closed to public scrutiny and does not respect basic civil freedoms, the freedom of speech. It is a system where each change of the ruling group is preceeded by a bloodbath.

A government imposed by a minority always leads to totalitarianism, is unable to rally round itself the best minds of the country, and, in the interest of consolidating power, is apt to destroy everything that constitutes the wealth of a society's thought, of human imagination, and is allegedly dangerous to the interests of "socialism" or of government. This is why I take the side of the communist Berlinguer, the communist Marchais, of the Spanish communists but not the side of the communist Brezhnev.

That is why an opposition is indispensable to our country — a legal opposition with equal rights and in accordance with the right of free association and assembly guaranteed by the Constitution. Political pluralism also finds expression in the indispensable freedom of professional unions, of consumer unions, of the press. If the Polish Socialist Party were still in existence we would be in a different situation. Pluralism need not at all mean tolerance of those forces which in the interest of a minority would wish to prevent economic, political, social renewal. Neither can there be tolerance for Fascism. But even when the bourgeoisie has been removed, a nation does not become uniform in world-wide outlook, nor uniform in a social, class, economic or an ideological sense. Development always comes about in the midst of contradictions, if I may use this much abused expression. Contradictions must be allowed to express and manifest themselves and the system of parliamentary democracy is the only one where this is possible. Despite undoubted drawbacks it is so far the only system of government tried through practice, which does not run counter to the will of the majority. Civil freedoms are essential prerequisites for social well-being and hence for the setting up of socialism. How many champions of social progress, how many socialist thinkers emphasised that socialism cannot be engendered nor cannot develop in a police-state which destroys free thought or, indeed, any thought differing from the officially accepted line.

An important social problem has arisen out of the nonsense of censorship, which has even outstripped tsarist censorship, crippling inter alia historical research, whenever it so much as alludes to the politics of by-gone Russia. One historian, for example, describes the capture and massacre of Praga* in

---

* the part of Warsaw on the east bank of the Vistula.

1794 in these words: "...and quite a proportion of the civil population suffered". This is done so as not to offend Russian chauvinist feelings. It brings to memory the XVIII century, times of shameless Russian interventions in Polish affairs.

Public access to information is drastically limited and the state of information to be found in officially available sources is leading to debility of social consciousness. There is not one newspaper in the country worthy of the name, information given on television and radio is simply scandalous in its awkwardness (a radio correspondent reports: "birds are flying over the fields and hedgerows"). The state the press is in, even the literary press, is simply lamentable, all through lack of freedom of the word and thought. Despite the resolutions of the Helsinki treaty the country is denied access to emigré publications which are of importance to national culture. Books by Gombrowicz, Miłosz or Kołakowski are confiscated. Western press is not on sale if it contains critical remarks about the USSR. The nonsense of these regulations is so blatant, that one cannot but ask who and what is it in aid of. Why does a political system feel endangered by 200 people reading critical remarks in "Le Monde"?

There has been a decline in social science. The official standing is that, for example, there is no need to seek new paths in economics and that only expert analysis is needed of so-called central problems of the national economic plan. Censorship, particularly the censorship of frightened editors, deletes any bold thinking that may be independent of the ossified imaginings of the "official" scientists. For this reason the social sciences cannot play the positive, stimulating role for which they are designated. In place of critical science a pseudoscience prevails which has an "ideological" character, i.e. amounts to propaganda. On the other hand, social science, if it is not a critical science, ceases to be a science altogether.

We all appreciate the achievements of the quinquennium after 1970 when at last the chalk circle of the fictions and superstitions of the previous period was broken. But there is no cause for optimism. The task of economic reform was undertaken, but in an inconsistent and undecided way because the conditions needed for an efficient working of the new principles laid down for the economy were not assured. The new system has been turned into an instrument for realizing inflationary processes. Instead of striving towards price checks by economic or even administrative means, increases concealed in one way or another were encouraged. Huge monopolistic organizations were set up, but no trouble was taken to create a market equilibrium which would give consumers the chance of even partly countering the monopolistic tendencies. Consumer organizations were not allowed to form. On the other hand, decisions on investment and other very important matters were made without public discussion and without exhaustive analysis of their effects. This led to even greater disturbance in the equilibrium of growth and to ever-growing chaos. We witnessed a great upsurge of spontaneity in the economy and the concomitant degradation of planning as the conscious control of economic processes. Under such circumstances any attempt at reforming the workings of the economy was doomed to failure. The reform was in practice abandoned in favour of a system of injunctions and prohibitions whose contradictions and ineffectiveness were revealed in the 50's and 60's.

Disquiet is also being caused by the heightening stratification of society, by the presence and growth of a strong privileged group and at the same time by the indisputable fact of real areas of need which are by no means small. Too little is being done to overcome the housing shortage, a need that is being combatted highly unsatisfactorily, just as unsatisfactorily as the growing plague of alcoholism. Both problems are extremely difficult and perhaps the means of solving them effectively are not yet available. I cannot fail to mention also the cancer of corruption.

A state of euphoria evoked by the achievements of the last quinquennium obscures from view the negative effects and censorship sees to it that knowledge of the areas of wrong stays unrevealed.

The aim of socialism is to satisfy the needs of man in such a way that man might really develop in all respects, might live well off and at the same time enrich himself spiritually, might actively participate in the life of society, so that he does not fall victim of the feeling that his life is bereft of meaning and sentences him to loneliness and blind vegetation in a sea of uncertainty and despair.

Socialism may not be decreed. It is and may only be born of the free action of free people. Hope is awakened by the fact that after thirty years of the political practices I have endeavoured here to describe, there are still people who have the courage to think and act.

I am deeply convinced that the movement of revival shall gain more and more in strength, that the recently intensifying repression will not contain it much longer, even though this repression is very dangerous to society and to the cause of socialism.

I cannot unfortunately limit my letter to generalities only. Our life abounds in too much nonsense, in too many human dramas for me to ignore them.

To this day a certain economist — a habilitated doctor — from Cracow is denied the possibility of carrying out scientific research ever since his dismissal during the anti-revisionist and anti-semitic purges in March 1968.

To this day Kołakowski, Brus and others who were deprived of their academic chairs in that same period, cannot continue their researches in this country.

The blacklist of persons prohibited from publishing and public appearance has recently grown longer including now the names of those of the writers, artists and scientists who signed or composed protests against the changes to the Constitution. Many signatories of these letters are being questioned by officers of the Security Service, some are faced with imminent dismissal from work or study, some are insulted, insinuations are made and provocations. The film director Jerzy Markuszewski, who, like me, signed the letter of the 59, has practically been prevented from carrying on his profession.

Many young people are offered confidential work for the Security Service, that is the highly paid work of informing on colleagues who hold unorthodox views. If they refuse, they are faced with dismissal from work, expulsion from study, reprisals.

Not so long ago a third-year student Jacek Smykał was expelled from the Pomeranian Medical Academy in Szczecin, without disciplinary hearing, for having debated points during classes in political science and then refusing to answer when questioned by the Security Service. Let me quote the official justification of the rector's decision: "... the accused expressed his views in the presence of thirty members of group D. The views, full of aggressive dynamism, recorded in testimonials, necessarily had a destructive influence on the outlooks and attitudes of his classmates, raising in the minds of his listeners unnecessary doubts and even evoking a distorted picture of, our reality. Moreover the accused showed passive resistance, assuming a nonchalant scornful air during questioning at the area H.Q. of the Militia thereby proving his complete lack of civil discipline towards employees of the security department."

In Lublin, Stanisław Kruszyński, a fifth-year student of the Catholic University of Lublin, is seriously ill in the investigative prison and for five months now awaits trial before a criminal court, accused of writing private letters to his wife and brother that had "disseminated false information which causes essential damage to the interests of the Polish People's Republic".

This year I am celebrating the 70th anniversary of my socialism. Nevertheless there is no room in a State which has decreed socialism for my reflections and experiences. I have been prohibited from giving lectures. I may not be quoted in the Press, and needless to say, my papers may not be published. The State Economic Publishers have stopped the printing of a book of mine which was to have been a jubilee edition.

Highly Respected Comrade First Secretary,
Poland is at present in a difficult situation, we have huge economic difficulties which are the result of growing chaos, inflation and the necessity of paying our foreign debts. We do not have an efficient system of managing the national economy. Our political system is anachronistic: it hinders positive selection of personnel preferring mediocrities and careerists, it checks all creativity in culture and science, produces feelings of frustration and indifference in people who are prevented from influencing the course of social events. We are a country that is dependent on a neighbouring power with all the consequences of this dependence.

Fundamental changes, or at least a clear-cut start on them, are a necessity. Otherwise we shall not avoid a tragedy which may take the shape of violent disturbances or a return to stalinist methods of ruling. The one and the other must at all costs be avoided for the sake of the elementary interests of the Polish nation, and for the sake of socialism. I believe that socialism remains the ideal which moulds the aspirations of the predominant part of our society. But this ideal will be eroded if social practice which calls itself socialist stays as it is today.

I know only too well, that even to make a beginning on essential changes is extremely difficult. I know how unrealistic at present is the chance of regaining complete sovereignty. But, I also know that certain positive changes are possible if only the leaders of our country found the courage, character and political sagacity to act in the interests of increasing our independence. In this effort they would find the full support of society, likewise would they find it for the democratic evolution of our political system. However, history will judge harshly those who place the nation's interest and the interests of socialism after their own convenience and after the group interests of power.

Edward Lipiński

Władysław Bieńkowski, born 1906, has from his youth played a prominent part in the communist movement. From 1956 to 1959 he was Minister of Education under Gomułka. In 1969, he was thrown out of the Party for writing a critical book on the way that Poland had developed after the Second World War. Two of his books have been published by the Polish emigré publishing house Institut Littéraire. The 1971 edition of the Polish Reference Encyclopaedia deleted his name from its entries.

OPEN LETTER TO THE AUTHORITIES OF THE POLISH PEOPLE'S REPUBLIC ON THE NORMALIZATION OF RELATIONS WITH THE SOVIET UNION

Relations with the Soviet Union are of fundamental importance to Poland on both a factual and an emotional plane. The Polish Nation will always preserve in grateful memory its liberation from nazi oppression and will never forget that the overthrow of Nazi Germany saved it from biological extermination; it also realizes that economic aid and co-operation with the Soviet Union was instrumental in raising it out of the ruins of war and later in successfully instituting a socialist economy. Both today and in the future the successful development of Poland depends in large measure on the development of comprehensive and friendly relations with our eastern neighbour. It is all the more an important problem for Poland to found these relations on a more permanent basis. The matter has all the more become relevant that the newly adopted Constitution of the Polish People's Republic places upon the State and the people, by hitherto unpractised custom, not only duties towards our own country but also a "duty of friendship" towards a neighbouring state. Since the provisions of a constitution go beyond state politics — they concern an area of much more sensitive issues: civic consciousness and sensibility — an all the more important and pressing task emerges of creating conditions which would make the provisions realizable, so that the citizens of the Polish People's Republic can in conscience be convinced that they are not breaking the law of their own land. This requires the exclusion from both the content and the form of our mutual relationship those factors which stand in the way of its development and upset its principal foundations. The favourable condition of our economy in recent years, which is justly described as strengthening the foundations of the socialist system exposes with even greater clarity how hampered are other areas and forms in the life of our country. It is a lame country and and a lame system whose economic development is not accompanied by developmment in intellectual and cultural life and by the development of scientific and political thought directed towards those problems of the State that are connected with both social system and society.

It is censorship that forms the basic obstacle in the internal life of the country. Fallacious and, as far as the ordinary man in the street is concerned, senseless conceptions of what may be harmful to the State or may endanger socialism, have resulted in removing from the sphere of intellectual activity problems and whole areas of social reality. The censorship to which our country has been subjected, interferes with everything — starting with ordinary information on current events, through the creative arts, journalism, right up to purely scientific works and dissertations, makes access to the scientific works of the world difficult for Polish science. Consequences of this have found drastic expression in the decline of Polish social thought and of all of the humanities. Polish sociology which ten years or so ago showed interesting symptoms of development and had a significant place in the world has been thrust into a state of complete marasma. Even in the most abstract areas of philosophy censorship ensures that nothing beyond what is in the official textbooks be written. Apart from our own office of censor, apart from the censoral duties

39

performed by the publishing houses themselves, the office of censor-in-chief is vested in the representative of the Soviet Union in Poland whose main task, it seems, is to be custodian of the ideological purity of an allied country and who, in not shirking from direct interference certainly makes no secret of his mission. Under pressure from him publication of books is stopped or books already published, which escaped the insufficiently watchful eye of our own censor, are withdrawn; sentences and complete portions of historical works are deleted even when they concern remote matters and particularly if they concern Polish-Russian relations, as though the Soviet authorities felt some solidarity with the policies of the Tzars. This is all too reminiscent of times, of just under two centuries ago, still fresh in the Nation's memory, when Poland, though still independent, was under the sway of the tsarist envoy. Relying on hirelings, on the might of the Russian army, on bribery and on promises of a political career, he depraved society, lent support to anarchy and nipped in the bud all attempts at healing the country.

Political common sense would require to avoid anything in our mutual relations that would have only one meaning to the Polish Nation: reference to a past that is tragic for us and inglorious to our friends. It would be naively misconceived to believe that concealment or falsication of the past would serve the purpose of normalizing our mutual relations. The objections or anxieties of Polish society lie rooted not in the past, which was erased by the October Revolution of 1956, but in the present and in fears for the future.

We have placed emphasis here on the fetters on intellectual and spiritual life, because all of the most essential problems of both the internal life of the country and of our mutual relations are concentrated in the issue of censorship as though it were a lens. It is exactly here that our differences are most distinctly expressed, differences in the course that the histories of our neighbouring countries took, differences of traditions which moulded the whole sphere of consciousness and emotional reaction. Ever since our history began, Russia knew only absolute despotic rule with uninhibited say-so, surrounded by complete secrecy, despotism that stiffled and repressed all sign of thought by means of a censorship perfected to legendary watchfulness. Poland never knew despotic rule or censorship in this sense (even under the "sanacja" government [of Piłsudski] in the inter-war years the abuses of the censorship which aroused the nation's indignation, were child's play compared with censorship on the lines of tzarist tradition). Suppression of information and fettered thought of this kind in Poland always meant only domination and occupation by foreign invaders. Hence, too, every attempt at imposing these methods on our country has alway met with vehement opposition from the whole of society and forced it to lead a double life whose spiritual (social, political) half is in a conspiracy not against the system or against socialism but against the nonsenses which are palmed off as socialism.

This difference of tradition found perspicuous expression in the discussion on the Constitution. The lively reaction and wide extent of interest in the issue should not come as a surprise — they result from the fact that Poland has the oldest democratic traditions in Europe (the Polish statute "neminem captivabimus" preceded the English "habeas corpus" act by 250 years) and from the fact that even those who did not study their country's history sucked traditions with their mother's milk. In consequence, thousands showed deep civil concern that this fundamental statute be given form and matter adequate for the needs of the Nation and consistent with its internal change. Abnormality in the atmosphere of political life only underlines the fact that the whole discussion of the constitution was withheld from society, that even proposals [put forward by the public] which were complied with were kept secret. What sounds altogether unbelievable — our authorities thought fit to resort to reprisals against the authors and signatories of discussion letters. The press published nothing but letters of praise (mainly written on the direction of the authorities) for the official proposals, whilst the views of major personalities and of custodians of the law showed goodness knows whether greater intellectual or moral decline.

From the point of view of Polish tradition the censorship imposed on our country may be treated as a relic of the Middle Ages which has nothing to do with safeguarding the State's interests, but on the contrary hinders development and exacerbates relations between society and the authorities. Perhaps for the citizens of the Soviet Union this kind of censorship is appropriate to strengthening their socialist convictions. Our difference in traditions comes to this, that in the eyes of the average Pole censorship can only compromise socialism.

At this point it is worth recalling Marx, who said that "censorship, like slavery, can never be law, though it may exist a thousand times in statutory form".

Just as it would be politically unwise not to take into account the different courses taken by history and the variously moulded traditions, so too, reference should be avoided to matters which in the past have been adjudged and condemned by the social conscience. This concerns our country too. It was, if only for this reason, an unforgivable crime of the previous party leadership committed against their own country to have allowed Poland's participation in the armed intervention in the internal affairs of Czechoslovakia in 1968, a participation that referred so directly to the ignominy and suicidal stupidity of the Polish politicians of 1938.

The basic political line taken by the party leadership of strengthening co-operation and friendship with the Soviet Union and the socialist countries is correct; it is consistent with the interests of the country and can count on the support of the whole of our society. But in following out these policies it is necessary to eliminate everything that is irreconcilable with friendship and co-operation. The realization of these policies cannot be entrusted to individuals — the likes of whom may be found in any country — who for the sake of their own careers outstrip each other in their servility towards a powerful neighbour and cause irretrievable damage to mutual relations. Society looks with disgust and contempt on the doings of such people, who vividly recall the examples of Targowica.* Their eagerness leads to such absurdities in point of view of constitutional law as the introduction of a duty of friendship towards the Soviet Union. This is not a directive for policy-making, in spite of attempts to represent it so. Polish policies have sufficiently many actual — political, economic and military — premises which are more categorically binding in effect than constitutional regulations.

The clause introduced into the constitution establishes a *legal status for international relations*, describes a *form of dependence* which nullifies all the claptrap about sovereignty that comes before. The Polish Nation is sufficiently aware of the Soviet Union's power status and holds out no hopes for

* Targowica — treacherous pro-Russian confederation in 1792 against the famous Constitution of May 3rd of 1791. The second partition of Poland was the direct consequence of the confederation.

real equality of rights. It is, however, the accepted custom in international relations that legal documents do not evidence the dependence of even the smallest nation on a super-power. This rule of decent conduct has been breached by the provision imposed in our constitution.

The only intention behind these remarks is the aim to found a permanent basis for friendship and co-operation between Poland and the Soviet Union, to remove and avoid all obstacles which might in the future produce disturbance and tension. The socialist countries have come out of their period of "trial and error" and have entered a phase which requires new and better forms to be found for the content which they have evolved — it is also necessary to find a more adequate basis and form for their mutual relations. The economic and military strength of the Soviet Union is a powerful arm in the socialist camp. It would be wrong, however, if force were the only tie linking the socialist countries.

Warsaw, March 1976.

Władysław Bieńkowski

Chapter three

YOUTH COMMITTEE
FOR THE IMPLEMENTATION
OF THE HELSINKI AGREEMENT

The first major European conference after the Helsinki summit was the European Youth and Students' Meeting held in Warsaw between 19 and 24 June 1976. 1500 delegates represented some 200 youth organizations from both the Eastern and the Western bloc. Hailed by the communist press as a "mini-Helsinki" it was to be at various moments as controversial as the original summit. For the first time an open letter prepared and distributed by an opposition group within one of the communist states was read out in open forum by a member of a Western delegation. In this document the "Polish Youth Committee for the Implementation of the Helsinki Agreement" listed various repressive measures, contravening the Final Act, which had been inflicted on a number of Polish students and young people. The document — in its original English — is reproduced in full after a brief description of the conference.

Aims and participation

The European Assembly of Youth and Students adopted as its slogan: "For Lasting Peace, Security, Co-operation, and Social Progress" which was the same as that used at the Helsinki summit in 1975. The purpose of the meeting was stated as being to provide a "broad forum" at which representatives of various political and ideological persuasions could discuss the possibilities and ways in which the younger generation could contribute to peaceful co-existence (as declared at Helsinki) and to display to the rest of the world the young Europeans' solidarity with "progressive forces" throughout the world.

There were a total of 34 countries represented, with some organizations like the Pan-African Youth Movement, the MPLA, UNESCO, World Peace Council, Unidad Popular Chilena, and the Ho Chi Min Working Youth Union having observers' status, which did not prevent them from voicing their opinions most fervently in the debates. The major international organizations which took part were: The Council for European National Youth Committees (CENYC), the European Federation of Liberal and Radical Youth (EFLRY), the International Union of Socialist Youth (IUSY), and the World Federation of Democratic Youth (WFDY). There was a noticeable absence of Conservative organizations, which was due to a disagreement on their representation at the Conference. Their absence led to a large political imbalance and a monopolization of the debates by what are generally known as "left-wing" forces.

The Conference

The procedure of the meeting took the form of main plenary sessions at the beginning and end of the Conference, with discussions taking place in five Commissions, each of which was supplemented by round-table discussions and seminars. Each Commission dealt with a particular aspect of the development of world peace and political stability. Human rights were discussed in Commission 3 and according to the programme took only a minor position in the agenda.

Although official reports were extensive, they failed to mention controversial or otherwise embarrassing questions that were tabled during the Conference. For instance, the solemn reading of Brezhnev's address during the first day of the Conference aroused strong disapproval from many of the Western participants. A further protest involved the German Federal Republic's National Youth Committee, who disputed the attempts to depict West Germany as a "country of injustice" and a factor "disturbing the re-establishment of social equity and peaceful co-operation" in Europe. There were some other mild attempts, for example, by a West German trade-unionist, who attacked the abuse of civil rights in Czechoslovakia, and the dismissal of workers for political reasons. There was also an interesting speech by a French Young Socialist, who asked the Soviet delegation to explain the persecution of the Jewish minority in the USSR. The Soviet representative replied "there was none". A number of differences in views were also apparent between the various communist representatives, which resulted in at least one serious and heated argument between the Soviet and Rumanian delegates concerning some unspecified issue. In many cases the serious ideological clashes were minuted as "incompatibility of views". A suggestion of the controversies was revealed in a report in the Polish Youth Federation's daily Sztandar Młodych (23 June), which denounced unspecified "attempts" by some Western delegates to "minimize the importance of the Helsinki Final Act."

Reading of the Open Letter

During the Conference, the English Young Liberal delegation made contact with an underground group in Warsaw calling themselves the Polish Youth Committee for the Implementation of the Helsinki Agreement. From them the Young Liberals obtained an open letter to the Conference, as well as a detailed brief of the situation in Poland, the

45

position of the main dissident forces: workers, students, intellectuals, and the Churches. The young Poles also explained why a large number of Polish citizens saw this particular Conference as a "sell-out" to the Soviets and why many more radical elements strongly disapproved of the discussions taking place at all. They explained that the whole Conference, as they saw it, had been pre-planned as a propaganda exercise and the fact that on the first day a personal message of goodwill from Leonid Brezhnev was read out, seemed to prove the point.

The Act which was to have such an effect on the Conference was the reading of the Open Letter by the Young Liberals, which they had received from the Polish Youth Committee. This letter was part of a speech delivered to Commission 3 when it dealt with the issue of human and civil rights. The speech itself was of particular interest as it went into some detail on the abuse of human and civil rights in both Czechoslovakia and the USSR. The case of Vladimir Bukovsky was dealt with at length, and the speaker quoted from Bukovsky's final remarks which he made at the trial in January: "Our society is still sick. It is sick with the fear we inherited from Stalin's terror. But the process of society's spiritual regeneration has already begun and there is no stopping it ... I will fight for legality and justice. And I only regret that during the brief period: one year, two months and two days when I was at liberty I managed to accomplish all too little towards that end." To this the Soviet delegation made no reply. They sat silently in the packed hall while the speaker continued to give examples: Mustafa Dzemilev, Dr. Semeon Gluzman, Zinoy Kasivsky, Andrei Tverdokhlebov, Pastor Jaromir Dus and Dr. Hejdenek. When the speaker turned to read the Open Letter, the Chair interrupted and insisted that his time on the rostrum had elapsed. Ignoring calls from the floor for an extension, a precedent which had been set by the Soviet and East German delegates, the Chair after consultations with the hosts again asked the speaker to step-down. As a mark of protest, the speaker left the hall to be followed by some 300 delegates.

The Conference organizers were faced with the forum being split and the whole Conference coming to an abrupt end. This was something they could not risk, and so, after half an hour of discussion with the Young Liberal delegation, the speaker was allowed to continue.

After this episode, there was the normal reaction, the speech was attacked as "reactionary", "anti-détente" and having "cold-war" overtones. However, having said this, one could not help but notice the change in attitude of the other delegates to the Young Liberals and to the Conference itself. Criticisms of Eastern Europe were not ridiculed and Western delegates began to be treated with more respect. The Polish and Soviet press discontinued front-page coverage of the Conference and it now occupied a minor position in the inside pages. Much of the final report of the Conference can be read as criticisms not only of Western Europe but also of Eastern Europe, especially the sections on economic issues, as well as human and civil rights.

Open Letter to the Participants of the Warsaw
Youth Conference — June 19–24 1976.

Dear friends,

Under the terms of the Final Act of the Conference for Security and Co-operation in Europe signed in Helsinki, the participating countries agreed to strive for a wider exchange of information and a better understanding of each other's problems. For this reason we wish to convey to you certain facts concerning the Youth of this country, acting as your hosts today. Since this information will not be made available to you from official sources, it remains for us to publicize it in this form.

Over centuries Poland has cherished a tradition of tolerance, freedom of speech and convictions. Alas, these freedoms are now constantly abused in the most drastic manner. Furthermore, in defiance of the terms of the Declaration of Human Rights and International Conventions of Human Rights, of which Poland is a signatory — political prisoners are often subjected to a treatment severely condemned in these documents.

It would be impractical to present to you a full dossier of all cases of abuse (information to that effect can be obtained from Amnesty International) but the following is a short list of last year's well-known trials:

1. Emil MORGIEWICZ, sentenced to 4 years' imprisonment for "circulating false information detrimental to the interests of the State", submitted a Memorandum to the Parliamentary Commission on the Penitentiary criticizing the conditions prevailing in the Polish prisons. Freed under pressure from public opinion in Poland and abroad, Morgiewicz lives under constant invigilation of security police.

2. Marian PIŁKA, Anna MORAWSKA, and Magdalena GÓRSKA, students at Lublin Catholic University, were arrested for billposting notices announcing a Requiem Mass for the workers killed during the riots on the Baltic Coast in December 1970. In his plea directed to the Prosecutor's Office Marian Piłka stated that during police interrogations his feet were trodden on by the policeman, he was kicked, abused and threatened with electric shock treatment.

47

3. Stanisław KRUSZYŃSKI, a theology student at the Catholic University of Lublin, has been sentenced to 10 months' imprisonment for expressing unorthodox political views in his private correspondence addressed to his wife, his brother and a close friend. The letters contained references to certain aspects of the present system of government, as well as known developments, such as e.g. a series of mysterious cases of arson discovered in Warsaw last year. The Court considered as "aggravating" circumstances the fact that during the search of his appartment the police found a number of books published abroad or in Poland before World War 2.

4. Two Warsaw schoolboys, Bernard KALINOWSKI (age 17) and Leszek MACIEJEWSKI (age 16) belonging to an informal discussion group called "Free Speech" were arrested under the charge of being the authors of... anti-Party graffiti on Warsaw's walls and fences.

5. Jacek SMYKAŁ, student at the State Medical Academy in Szczecin, at the request of the dean was relegated from Poland's student body on the grounds of "publicly expressing views which may have a 'destructive' effect on the outlook and stance of his colleagues, provoking unnecessary confusion in their minds". He was also accused of "demonstrating passive resistance and a nonchalant attitude" during police interrogation. In fact, Smykał's "offence" was that during a political science seminar he asked a question on the numerical strength of the police and security forces in Poland. He also refused indignantly an offer made to him during the interrogation of signing a declaration of loyalty.

These are just a few of the most recent cases. We should also mention that in the years 1968–1969 a series of political trials took place in Poland at which sentences of up to several years' imprisonment were imposed on students. During the police interrogations the students were beaten, slandered and abused. In 1970 a severe sentence was passed in the case of young people accused of importing Western books into Poland. In 1971 the Courts were busy again sentencing members of the so-called "Ruch" organization, an informal group striving for greater democratization of the political system in Poland. The longest prison term was seven years.

Young people are usually arrested and charged according to paragraph 78, art. 271 (sometimes in conjunction with art. 273) of the Penal Code referring to "membership of a clandestine organization", or "spreading and circulating false information detrimental to the interests of the Polish State". Informal discussion groups or debating societies assembling without official sponsorship of the two government- and Party-directed Youth Organisations (SZMP and SZP) are qualified by the police and the judiciary as "clandestine organisations". By the same token, criticism of government, its policies, political system or even Party-Government decisions expressed at these meetings comes under "circulating false information" clause.

Just recently we have created a Polish Youth Committee junction with similar Committees set up in Western and Eastern Europe, USA and even USSR will keep a watch on the signatories' commitment to carry through the Provisions of the Final Act.

We are in no position to foresee if the authorities will not prosecute us for passing this document containing true and accurate information. However, we appeal to you, dear Friends — and especially to visitors coming from countries where all criticism and all opinions are expressed freely — to demonstrate your solidarity with our cause as effectively as you are doing it in respect of young people persecuted by other dictatorial and totalitarian régimes around the world.

We call for your solidarity and support in the cause of freedom, justice and human rights, the ideals which inspire the youth of the world today.

Polish Youth Committee
for the Implementation of
Helsinki Agreement

This was by no means the only letter to be produced by the said Committee. Later documents (which, for reasons of limited space, cannot be reproduced here) include a letter supporting the Workers' Defence Committee and an Open Letter addressed to the participants of the Belgrade Conference.

Chapter four

THE EVENTS OF JUNE 1976
AND THEIR IMMEDIATE AFTERMATH

The first wave of workers' protests

In June 1976 widespread strikes almost toppled the Party leadership. The strikes were a decisive reaction to the authorities' attempts to increase substantially the prices of a number of basic commodities. The irony of this was that Edward Gierek had become Party leader in December 1970 in similar circumstances, when his predecessor, Władysław Gomułka, tried to push through a 25% increase in food prices and was forced to resign in the face of massive revolt. It was only the complete climb-down by the authorities in 1976 which kept them in power. However the long-term political consequences of the June events were far more important since they led to the formation of an organized "opposition" movement embracing different social strata (the term "opposition" is in some ways a misnomer since the movement's aim is to make the authorities genuinely respect their own laws).

The attempt to increase prices

On Thursday 24 June, the Polish Premier, Mr. Piotr Jaroszewicz, gave details in Parliament and on television of a series of price increases. Sugar was to go up by 100%, meat and fish by 69%, butter and better quality cheeses by 60%, poultry and vegetables by 30%. This would have added 39% to the food bill of an average family and thereby increased total household expenditure by some 16%. The people, according to Mr. Jaroszewicz, had been consulted and the increases were to take effect from the following Monday.

Price increases had been expected; they were foreshadowed at the VII Party Congress in December 1975. The authorities had been spending very large sums to keep food prices at 1970 levels and were now anxious to reduce the subsidy. In practice, articles were being repackaged or renamed and then sold at higher retail prices. At the same time there were continual shortages of meat since so much of it was exported to pay for the huge imports of Western manufactured goods. Moreover, consumer goods industries, including agriculture, which is mostly in private hands, have deliberately had a lower and insufficient level of investment as compared with capital goods industries.

The proposed increases were far greater than had been previously intimated and so large that it was clear that their aim was not primarily to alter the structure of food prices but rather to change the pattern of consumption. Some items, notably meat, which has always been an important part of the staple diet, would in fact become too expensive to be purchased in the same quantities as in the past. A system of food vouchers and bonuses was simultaneously to be instituted, but this compensation favoured those on higher salaries — who tended to be Party members — since they received more in absolute terms. Also there were obnoxious strings attached, for example, a change of employment would entail a loss of bonuses.

The strikes

Strikes and demonstrations broke out the next morning on Friday 25 June. The population was angered by the severity of the increases and the fictitious nature of the consultations. Demands were made to see Party officials. There was some violence, a traction engine was derailed outside the Ursus Tractor Plant near Warsaw and the Party headquarters was ransacked in Radom. Strikes took place in Katowice, Łódź, Opole, Olsztyn, Poznań, Warsaw and Wrocław. A general strike was imminent.

The authorities had expected protests and had taken various precautionary measures. In May, in a number of coastal towns (which had seen bloody riots in 1970) many policemen underwent training in crowd control. On about June 20th, rumours circulated in Gdynia and Gdańsk to the effect that thousands of young dockers had been suddenly called up for army exercises. In Łódź, one of the most important industrial cities in Poland, the Mayor signed a series of instructions providing for "accelerated proceedings", i.e., hasty trials and summary justice in any of a long series of crimes involving demonstrations, public disturbances and vandalism. These instructions were to have been announced over the radio, but, fifteen minutes before the broadcast was to take place, the transmission was cancelled. Thus the general public were unaware of this directive, even though it was legally binding on them. These examples clearly illustrated the fictitious nature of the consultations which Mr. Jaroszewicz said had taken place: such precautions would have been totally unnecessary if the population had been involved in a genuine dialogue and if their agreement had been secured.

On the evening of the 25th Mr. Jaroszewicz re-appeared on television and stated that, in view of "valuable amendments and contributions" put forward by the working class, the increases were being withdrawn until a later date. That date still remains unspecified.

As soon as the Premier made his announcement, the protests stopped and those involved began to disperse. It was then that the security organs launched a wave of reprisals harking back in severity to the Stalinist era. Strikers and innocent bystanders were savagely beaten in the streets and in jails. They were then tried by courts where the official legal procedure was ignored. Many workers were dismissed and could not find other employment for a long time. Not a single official body showed any concern for those workers and their families who were deprived of any means of subsistence.

In these circumstances both the Polish Catholic Hierarchy and many well-known intellectuals championed the cause of the workers. Appeals were sent to the Polish authorities. Distinguished individuals abroad were also asked to express their support for workers' rights. Many did so (Heinrich Böll, Gunther Grass, Enrico Berlinguer, Jean-Paul Sartre to mention but a few).

EYE-WITNESS ACCOUNTS

At first, information about the scale of the strikes and the official reaction was sketchy. One of the first detailed reports to be smuggled to the West described what happened to the workers employed at the Ursus Tractor Plant on the outskirts of Warsaw.

A REPORT OF REPRISALS AGAINST THE WORKERS OF THE URSUS AND OTHER MOTOR WORKS
(Based on numerous eye-witness accounts)

On 25 June almost the whole of the labour force of the Ursus Motor Factory was on strike from morning. At first the workers waited on the shop floor for the management representatives to come and at about 9 a.m. made their own way out of the factory to the administrative block. The workers demanded that the representatives of the principal authorities come immediately for consultations with the labour force of the factory. This demand was refused by the management and, in view of this, workers took positions on nearby railway lines and stopped rail traffic on the Warsaw to Kutno and Warsaw to Skierniewice lines. The purpose of this action was to inform as large a number of people as possible of the Ursus strike.

Protest action was throughout carried out in quite an orderly fashion. Police authorities did not intervene, but only mobilised large units of militia and kept observation (including helicopter surveillance). Of the more important incidents mention should be made of the following: a female worker slapped the local Party First Secretary and the Ursus Manager when, during their address to the crowd, they were critical of the strike; trains were stopped, including international connections; railway lines were dismantled and an unsuccessful attempt was made at cutting the rails with acetylene torches; a traction engine was rolled into the gap where the rails were taken up; an egg delivery van was stopped and the eggs were distributed among the strikers and casual passers-by; a sugar-delivery van was stopped and the sugar partially distributed.

About 8 p.m. the workers heard a television broadcast by the Premier revoking the price increases and after this announcement they began to disperse. It was precisely at this moment that detachments of militia attacked the dispersing crowds with rockets and tear gas, hitting out with truncheons and kicking those who had fallen. During the police action a restaurant car burst into flames (probably hit by a rocket or other incendiary device). The fire was extinguished by the factory fire brigade but because of difficult operational circumstances (successive charges by police detachments) the restaurant car and part of the next coach were destroyed.

The militia detachments then organized a man-hunt that was accompanied by the brutal beating of people in the streets, mainly of youths. Both uniformed and the plain-clothes detachments rounded up people, often passers-by, in the area round the factory, in the town's main streets and on the outskirts of Ursus. Those stopped were beaten with truncheons, spanners, belt buckles and were kicked often to unconsciousness. This operation lasted until morning.

Here are some examples illustrating the methods used by the police authorities:

— a worker on his way for the third shift was arrested and brutally beaten;
— a worker returning from the second shift was arrested and beaten and physically maltreated in a police car;
— a worker who had gone to fetch his wife, on foot, from [nearby] Włochy (from the second shift) was arrested and beaten up in his wife's presence; he was dragged by the feet to a police car;
— a worker returning home with his wife in late pregnancy was forcibly pushed into a police car, his wife having been thrust aside;
— a worker returning in the evening to the workers' hostel was stopped near the hostel by some men in civilian clothes driving a private car (commandeered for the operation) and was beaten in the car until he was bleeding;

— some young people walking near a police station along the
Street of the Heroes of Warsaw were attacked by militia
and beaten; one of them lost consciousness, whereupon
he was abused as he lay unconscious; he was later picked
up by an ambulance;
— a young worker was hit so hard with a truncheon during
the police intervention that he sustained fractures of the
skull in two places.

On arrival at the Ursus police station the arrested had
to run the gauntlet between a double line of policemen who
thrashed them with truncheons. Some were forced through the
double line twice. Once inside the building, they were thrown,
one by one, into a special room where a number of policemen
would beat them and kick them and if some fell they would
be kicked on the ground. Cases are known where ribs were
broken. In the back yard of the station a "health trot" was
organized: those under arrest were ordered to run round the
yard under a hail of truncheons.

It seems that all the arrested were beaten — not one
exception to this rule is known. That night a sum total of
200 to 300 people were arrested.

The arrested were next transported to the Mostowski
Palace [in Warsaw] — those who had collapsed during the
beating were dragged by their feet and forcibly thrown into
the police cars. In the Mostowski Palace they were photo-
graphed and had their fingerprints taken. Then they were
examined under ultra-violet lamps to see if they had been
marked with special dust dispersed by cartridges fired for
identification purposes during the earlier action by the police.
Here too the first interrogations were carried out. Then they
were transported to the police headquarters in Rakowiecka
Street. Before being taken to the Mostowski Palace some had
a stop-over at the Walicόw police station, where they were
also beaten.

On Sunday 27th June Special Tribunals were called and
these sat late into the night. Those arrested were charged
with attacking the police, ignoring orders to disperse, demolishing shops, railway carriages, etc. The majority of the
accusations were false. Policemen were called as witnesses —
generally these were not the same people as had arrested the
accused — and cases were heard based on written evidence
submitted by absent witnesses for the prosecution.

Almost all the accused were sentenced. Fines and penalties between 1500 and 5000 zlotys were meted out, or some dozen hours of unpaid community work, or suspended imprisonment. After 48 hours most of the accused were sent home.

On Monday 28 June workers who had been sent home resumed work, though some had to stay at home suffering from shock as a result of the beatings. After a few days the Motor Works terminated without notice contracts of employment of all those workers who had been arrested, citing as legal grounds Article 52 §I of the Penal Code. Those of them who had accommodation at the workers' hostel were ejected from their lodgings the following day.

It was primarily those who had been arrested who were dismissed from work. Nevertheless a much wider group was subject to dismissal. Dismissals were handed out on the basis of photographs taken by the police and on the basis of statements made by some of the managers and informers. In the course of this, workers' rights were blatantly violated. Here are some examples:

— a worker who had been off sick for a long period and had a medical certificate of exemption from work, had his contract of employment terminated without notice; on 25 June this worker had not even been at work on account of illness;

— another worker's contract was similarly terminated though he was on holiday at the time and had not even been to work on that day.

Since on 25 June almost everyone at Ursus had been on strike the management could dismiss anyone they themselves or the supervisory staff did not like. The total number of dismissed at the Ursus plant is not known. Various figures are quoted. One quite frequent estimate puts the figure at 250 and another at about 1500. This divergence has hitherto not been clarified — one should expect confirmation of the second rather than the first estimate.

Between 4 and 6 July those of the workers who had been sentenced to fines were served summonses to appear at the Ursus police station. They presented themselves thinking that only formalities of some sort were required. However, they were arrested and taken to Warsaw to the police headquarters on Rakowiecka Street (this included persons who had paid their fines). It turned out that the Warsaw Police Command had ordered a revision of the earlier sentences, which it considered too lenient. The Special Tribunals were directed to re-hear all cases and return sentences of absolute imprisonment. That was indeed the way that matters went and now almost all sentences came to three months' imprisonment. Some of the cases were tried with complete disregard for the principles laid down by the Code of Penal Proceedings. Thus for example, statements by an absent witness (witness Dynda) were cited at the trial which alleged that the accused had attacked policemen. The Court gave no credence to denials by the accused and based their verdict on just the written evidence of the prosecution witness, who was not present at the trial. Often use was made of an indirect witness for the prosecution (witness Dąbek) who had merely put on record at the police station personal details of those arrested and the cause of arrest as stated by the police escort. Since witness Dąbek had not recorded personal details of the police escort, there was no way of checking the credibility of the information. It happened too that witnesses confused various of the accused and did not know at all well where they had made their arrest.

After hearing their sentences workers were transferred to the Białołęka prison. Many of them submitted appeals, unsuccessfully, as a rule, because the second hearings had confirmed the earlier verdicts. The Court also made no reaction to statements by workers that they had been beaten by the police.

When the first month was up, some of those sentenced (about 40 in number) were offered suspension of the remaining two months of imprisonment for a period of 6 months. Thus about 40 people were released from prison at the beginning of August. It is worth noting that those who had earlier paid their fines and had then been sentenced again (to three months' imprisonment) have still not received their money back. They were thus punished twice for the same actions.

All those workers who faced reprisals (this applies both to those who had only been dismissed from work as well as those who had been tried) can find no employment anywhere. State employers, co-operatives and even private employers have been banned from accepting them into employment (private employers were threatened with suspension of their licences). The Warsaw Employment Bureau will not even agree to interview workers dismissed from work as a result of events of 25 June. In some cases workers who had been accepted (despite the ban) were dismissed from their jobs. The Area Review Committee in Pruszków as of now still takes a negative view of applications for a review of dismissal decisions. Workers are convinced that they will have lost continuity of employment and related rights.

On 16 and 17 July, the County Court in Warsaw tried seven workers accused of derailing a traction engine. Five of them worked at the Ursus Motor Works, one at the nearby Pruszków machine tool factory and one was a truck driver who also ran a newspaper kiosk for "Ruch". None of them had any previous convictions. The youngest was not quite 21, the eldest was 42 years old. They were officially assigned legal counsel. The only evidence available consisted of photographs. Sentences were handed out of 5 years, 4 and a half years, 4 years and 3 years imprisonment. The highest sentence was given to the youngest of the accused. Most of the families of these accused are in dire financial straits:
— Grzegorz Zielonka (aged 42) left a wife with two adopted children aged 7 and 8; the wife has to look after a sick and disabled mother, so she cannot take up employment; the family thus has no means of support;
— Czesław Milczarek (aged 27) left a wife and two children (1 and 3 years old); the wife looks after a mother who suffers from severe asthma; nevertheless she has decided not to stop working;
— Wojciech Czarniecki left a mother who recently underwent a partial gasterectomy; the mother receives a State pension of 900 zlotys.

In August two trials were held at the Pruszków Court of persons accused of distributing eggs and sugar from the smashed delivery vans. Altogether 12 people were sentenced to jail for from 1 year's suspended sentence to between 3 and 5 years' imprisonment. The families of those convicted are also suffering severe material hardship.

The number of workers still detained remains unknown. It is thought the number reaches 50. Some of these (10 persons) are the subject of an investigation regarding derailment of a locomotive. Some of their families experience severe material difficulty:

— a family with a large number of children (aged between 4 and 15); the wife cannot seek employment for health reasons; they do not have any means of living and receive some, though inadequate, help from relatives;

— aged parents, both gravely ill (mother blind and suffering from severe diabetes, father with bilateral hernia); their elder son came out of prison after six weeks' detention and still faces proceedings; he is severely ill with a deformed spine and diabetes and this year suffered three heart attacks (in May, June and also early July during beatings at the police station in Ursus); the younger son's arrest was extended by the Public Prosecutor to October and he is in Mokotów prison; as a result of beatings by the police he sustained fractures of the jaw in two places;

— to this moment a young boy who is mentally retarded and has been receiving medical attention since infancy is under detention (since the beginning of July) pending investigation

Help from places of work and local Social Security offices is feeble. Allowances which a place of employment is legally bound to pay and which were approved at the lower administrative level were rejected by an over-riding authority. Also, local social workers refuse to help when approached. Since for the most part families were supported by the present victims of the reprisals, they are now themselves deprived of medical care.

Note: the above account contains names of only those who have so far been tried in cases reported by the press. Names of other persons mentioned are known to the authors of this account. The names are not disclosed here for fear of further reprisals that might be applied to the persons concerned.

Information Bulletin No. 1, an unsigned samizdat, which started to circulate in September 1976, was the first to bring eye-witness accounts of the incidents in Radom. It was some time, however, before a clearer picture emerged. A much later issue of the same Bulletin (No. 8, dated February 1977) carried three detailed reports, this time signed. They were the fruit of investigations made by private individuals (collaborators of the Workers' Defence Committee, cf. Chapter 5), who despite considerable police harassment, helped the victims of reprisals and attended court hearings. Below is an extract of a report of the incidents, followed by an article which depicts the atmosphere in Radom prior to the strikes and describes some of the trials.

The introduction to the Bulletin, repeated in each issue, is cited first because of its important message:

The aim of this bulletin is to break the state monopoly of information, protected by the existence of censorship. The information it contains serves the cause of openness in public life and constitutes a chronicle of reprisals both against the citizens of this country and against its culture and heritage. By disseminating this bulletin you are acting within your rights, and playing a part in their defence.

Read it, copy it, and pass it on. Expose cases of violation of civil rights. Remember — by destroying this bulletin, you are sealing your own lips, and those of others.

EDITORIAL COMMITTEE

RADOM, JUNE 1976

On the morning of 25 June the Walter Metal Works went on strike. According to a number of accounts a management representative went to the F-6 Department on hearing about the stoppage. There he was showered with questions about the proposed price increases which he was unable to answer; he began to back out. The workers followed him, and the workers from other departments joined them. A considerable crowd (of over 1000, according to some accounts) gathered in the courtyard. A strike was announced, and it was decided to inform the whole of Radom about it. Representatives of the Walter workers made their way to other plants on battery-powered trucks. Before 10 a.m., a procession was formed outside the Walter Works, which then marched out towards the Party headquarters. By about 10 a.m., several thousand people had gathered outside the Party building. They demanded answers to their questions concerning the planned price increases. The Regional Secretary tried to talk to those assembled through a megaphone. A small number of hand-outs was circulated explaining the principles of wage compensation, and a reply to the queries was promised in approximately two hours' time. The people outside the headquarters waited. Many new people joined the crowd during this period, while some left and went back to their places of employment. At about noon a handful of people entered the building, but apart from lower-ranking staff and some plain-clothes policemen they found no one. This caused indignation among the people in the crowd. Stones began to be thrown, and a number of windows were broken. (None of my informers directly witnessed the undressing of one of the Regional Party Secretaries, although many had heard of this incident.) Several people got into the buffet in the building. They started taking cold meat, sausages and tinned ham outside and, showing it to the demonstrators, shouted: "...look at the way these guzzlers live! ...And what about us?..." The crowd began to invade the building. At about 1 p.m. a systematic ransacking of the building began. Television sets, desks and armchairs were thrown out through the smashed windows. At about 3 p.m. a fire was started on the ground floor, in the hall by the cloakroom. The demonstrators did not let the fire brigade in. Barricades were in all likelihood erected in First of May Street to hinder the passage of fire engines, and that is when the unfortunate death [of T. Ząbecki, see p. 100] under the wheels of a tractor or trailer took place. Casualties were placed on a battery-operated truck and taken to the Regional Hospital. One of the smaller fire engines was set on fire, and the road surface began to burn as well. Both these fires were put out relatively swiftly.

All this took place in the vicinity of the Party headquarters. At this time the rest of the town was still relatively quiet. Then a handful of people armed with large sticks appeared on Żeromski Street, making their way down from shop to shop and systematically breaking all the windows. No one hindered them in this. Why did the police not intervene? The main body of demonstrators was on First of May Street near the Party building; there were few people on Żeromski Street, and a small number of policemen could have put a stop to the damage being done there without much difficulty. In fact, however, long before the rioting, at about 10 a.m., all policemen were instructed to put on plain clothing and watch the demonstrators incognito. They took photographs and filmed everything that took place in the streets. Thus there were no policemen to step in on Żeromski Street. Neither the Regional nor the Supreme Court sentenced anybody for the systematic damage of shop windows.

At approximately 5 p.m. the crowd began to throw goods out of the damaged shops. Looting and wrecking commenced. The wooden scaffolding on Żeromski Street was broken and overturned. The street looked as though it had been barricaded along its entire stretch. It was then that the motorized division of the police, which had been waiting at Radom airport since noon, received an order to intervene. They had not been there at 12 noon, when the demonstrators stood outside the Party building, nor at 3 p.m. when the headquarters was on fire; they attacked when the looting began. This was purely a tactical move, since plain-clothes policemen had been arresting demonstrators "on the quiet" since much earlier on. The first detainees were taken to the Regional Police head-quarters at 12 noon, long before the wrecking and setting fire to the Party building. By 7 p.m., the town had become quiet again. It was completely taken over by the police. That day huge numbers of people were detained. Only a tiny fraction of these were the ones who had looted and stolen. This deficiency of criminals in the police cells was particularly inconvenient for the security authorities, and gave rise to a number of procedures whose purpose was to increase the number of people suspected of stealing. These procedures have been described in complaints submitted to the Public Prosecution Department of the Polish People's Republic after the sentences had come into force. There were three variants of the action taken up by the police to cast suspicion on innocent people:

1. People detained earlier were driven around the town in a car and made to pick up various objects scattered around the street. The car would return to the police station with ready-made "pilferers" and "evidence of the crime".

2. Beating was used to force confessions of having stolen objects which were already in the police station.

3. Incidental passers-by were stopped (after 8 p.m.) and compelled, by threats of beating or murder, to take a parcel; after they had walked a short distance with the parcel, they would be stopped again with the "stolen goods" in their possession.

This modus operandi was not, however, very widespread, and was used on a maximum of some 30 people.

Approximately 2000 people are estimated to have been detained on 25th June and the following several days. Some of them appeared before the Court or Magistrate within 48 hours, charged with violating Article 51 of the Minor Offences Code. The decision as to who would be tried by the Court and who by the Magistrate was arbitrary. The Magistrates initially sentenced defendants to several days' community work, then to fines, and later still to two or three months' jail. Occasionally, the same person would be up before the Magistrates three times, a different sentence being passed each time. The Court sentences were all to several months' imprisonment. All those who were not sentenced to a term in jail were released from custody on 27 or 28 June; some of them returned to stand trial a few days later. By that time a new group had joined the list of detainees: people who had previous records in the police files and who did not necessarily take part in the events of 25 June, but whose past justified the terms "hooligans", "squabblers", "dregs of society". Many people were arrested on the basis of anonymous denunciations. There were also cases of witnesses, whose names had been given by defendants to prove that they had not looted or wrecked, being brought in and indicted. Arrests lasted for three weeks after the demonstrations. During this period many homes were searched, and arrests were made of all those whose premises had been searched irrespective of what was found on them. If nothing could be pinned on such a person he would be charged with participating in the riots or with verbal assault of a police officer. Many were charged with stealing or accepting stolen goods. Nonetheless, it is my conviction that even despite the unprincipled statements made by the testifying police officers it would have been very difficult to indict the majority of those accused if the authorities had not adopted the principle of collective responsibility. All the demonstrators were charged with the offence that "in Radom on the day of the 25th June they took part in a rowdy street gathering whose participants joined forces in a violent assault on public officers and on public objects and amenities, in the consequence of which they caused bodily harm to 75 police officers and damage to public property to the value of over 28 million zlotys" (this quotation is to be found in every indictment). Such a formulation allowed the authorities to bring to trial anyone who had even for a moment found himself in the street, i.e. in effect any citizen of Radom. By making everyone responsible for assaulting the 75 policemen and causing 28 million zlotys' worth of damage, nothing needed to be

62

proven except presence in the street, and this was indeed the sole procedure of the prosecution in many of the trials I attended.

Approximately 300 cases were heard in all at the Regional Court in Radom (as the court of first instance) after the June events; the number of defendants, however, did not exceed 200. This indicates that not many short of 100 people were tried twice for the same offence — under the Minor Offences Code at the end of June, and under the Penal Code after August. About 100 people in all were convicted of theft. The County Court in Radom sentenced 25 people in the first instance; those cases were then taken to the Supreme Court in Warsaw. At the end of July 1976 almost all the decisions of the Magistrates' Courts were questioned by the Regional Prosecution Department in Radom and brought in for recon‑sideration. (Those sentenced returned home after a month in jail.) Subsequent sentences were to fines of between 500 and 2,000 zlotys.

Mirosław Chojecki

RADOM ON TRIAL

One can get from Warsaw to Radom within two hours. Trains run every few hours and there are frequent buses. The town has over 70,000 inhabitants. It has been a large industrial centre since before the war. The Polish Socialist Party was traditionally the strongest organization there. Many families still relate accounts of pre-war strikes and rallies. At present Radom has a considerable number of factories and industrial plants, including several large concerns.

What immediately strikes a newcomer to Radom is the contrast between the plan of the town and its real picture. The wide streets of the town centre, with their restaurants and hotels, create the aura of a metropolis; but one need not even leave the main street, Żeromski Street, to see — having walked through the front door of any one of the blocks, and out of the back — a neglected yard, some ramshackle wooden sheds serving as living quarters, outside lavatories. A flat will often consist of one room for five or six people, with a cubby-hole of a kitchen. Several minutes' journey from the station, just past "Radoskór", a factory which employs several thousand people, is the Gliwice district, built in the 1920s:

small single-storey houses, streets without cobblestones or lighting. To this day there are streets in other districts of Radom — such as Kozia Góra or Oboziak — where water is delivered by cart. Electricity, alone of the achievements of the 20th century, has penetrated into these areas, in the form of TV sets and badly-lit streets.

Some 70,000 people lived in Radom before the war; now, industry alone employs 50,000. New districts and estates have admittedly been built (the largest proportion from the funds of the Walter Metal Works): Planty, Piętnastolecia, Malczewskiego; most of the accommodation there, however, was taken by arrivals from outside Radom. The housing programme has definitely been insufficient for the needs of this expanding town. Families can wait for over 15 years for a flat, while there is a 12-year waiting list in the housing co-operatives.

The principle applied to the building of factories seems to have been "the more the quicker, the better". In 1963 a new plant manufacturing sewage equipment was opened in the Potkanów district: "Łączniki". Work in some of the departments is so hard that employees leave after only three or four months. This factory always has vacancies. When, after 25 June, almost no plant or factory was willing to take on the "brawlers" and "squabblers" who had been sacked, "Łączniki" employed all who volunteered for the work.

The average wage in Radom is one of the lowest in Poland. Privately employed workers have relatively high earnings — they, however, were described in the indictments as "casuals". By this criterion, the entire working class described by the classic writers of Marxism consisted of "casuals".

The model that is put forward in most Polish studies of the working class is one of advancement and climbing up the ladder, whether economic, social or cultural, connected partly with the influx of labour from the villages. By this paradigm, the son of an unskilled labourer remains unskilled himself solely through bad fortune, lack of ambition, or lack of ability. Such a theory finds no confirmation in Radom. Deprived of independent political or trade union organizations, the workers are unable to oppose their conditions of work. The erosion of traditional values has frequently led here to degradation. The line separating the "real workers" from the "dregs of society" — from what used to be called the lumpenproletariat — is becoming increasingly less distinct. The workers and the non-workers live in the same type of home, go out to the same type of yard, drink in the same bars, buy their vodka after hours in the same drinking-dens. Recently, Radom's only theatre was closed down. Television is the most popular form of cultural entertainment. Time spent in jail or in a sobering chamber, or a fine from the Magistrate are so frequent that it is impossible to speak of deviation from the norm. It is difficult to give a reason for this state of affairs: it could derive from the indolence of the social policy, or from the deliberate destruction of independent working class traditions.

In December 1975 a trade union meeting took place in one of the Radom factories. Initially, it ran along typical lines: boring, meaningless speeches, fruitless discussion. Then a worker with nearly 30 years' experience spoke up. He said that if there were no change in the attitude to the workers and their needs, the coming year in Radom would see a repetition of the situation on the Baltic Coast in December 1970. The worker put his job in jeopardy with this statement; things were calmed down, but in June he was one of the first to be dismissed.

Even at the beginning of June there were go-slows and temporary stoppages in the Walter Metal Works. The immediate reasons for this were a disadvantageous change in the norms that had to be fulfilled, and the fact that compensation was not paid out to a female worker who had had an accident at work. Afterwards, a certain number of people were sacked. It is difficult to project the Radom experiences onto the country as a whole. At the end of June 1976, there was a strike throughout Poland. The increase in food prices became an unprearranged call-word for stopping work. I should like to take issue at this point with the popular theory that this was merely a reaction against the fall in the standard of living. Naturally, this factor should not be underestimated. For working-class families with many children the increase would have been materially disastrous. The example of Radom goes to prove, however, that the June events were also an attempted struggle for dignity.

The picture which emerges from the various accounts of the Walter Works employees is one of a factory in which conditions are not so different from those on a feudal estate. The manager, Mr. Błoński, had a habit of "lying in wait" behind a piece of machinery on the shop floor. If he saw the slightest irregularity — such as a spanner replaced incorrectly — he would deduct a percentage from the worker's bonus. If he noticed that an employee did not work for, say, fifteen minutes, he would sack him. The guiding principle seems to have been to cause division and conflict between the workers and their immediate superiors. After 25 June, verification commissions were set up in the Radom factories. They consisted of the senior foreman in the given department and of Party activists. The foreman had to detail candidates for talks with the commission. In the Walter Works, each department received a quota of people it had to dismiss. The size of the quota depended on the management's assessment of the degree of activity displayed by the particular department in the strike. In the F-6 Department, where the strike probably began, there were cases of entire work teams being sacked. A petty denouncement — "...called on people to stop work... shouted... took part in the demonstration..." — was sufficient to have an employee dismissed. If a foreman refused to take on the role imposed on him by management, there would be attempts to dismiss him, too, or he would be moved to another post.

The trade unions likewise had a specific task to carry out in penalising the workers. In one of Radom's largest factories the son of a worker who had been sacked (after 25 years of employment) was crossed off the list of workers' children going to summer camp. The child's mother, employed at the same factory, appealed to the Works Council. She was told that the son had to take the consequences for his father's action. Repeated requests for a change of decision caused the official to ring up the senior foreman in the mother's department. After a brief exchange of words he told her: "You're lucky. The foreman gave you a good reference. As an exceptional case, your son can go to camp".

The attitude of the technical supervisors and engineers at the head of the departments also gives cause for concern. Their behaviour after the June events may partly be explained by fear; but the hostility they displayed towards their subordinates in dismissing them and then testifying against them in appeal commissions and labour courts is indicative of a far more deeply rooted process. They have learnt to treat workers like mindless children — a mere labour force with no will of its own. They saw the June strike as a rebellion against their authority and privileges. Most of them were given at least their secondary and higher education in the Polish People's Republic.

The authorities reacted to the workers' rebellion like an enraged landlord. Pretexts for their reprisals were provided by the looting and damage to property. The participation of drunkards in the demonstration was also particularly stressed. What was, however, a superfluous appendage to the demonstration has been presented as its very essence. I do not intend to justify the thoughtless actions which accompanied the June protest. It is necessary, however, to understand why a fury seized certain people in Radom in the late afternoon on 25 June. The demonstrators had been waiting since the morning for the authorities' answer to their postulates. Tension rose; some tried to dispel it by drinking. The protesting workers received no reply. Even before the announcement that the increases were to be withdrawn, some of the people began to make their way home. On their way back, along Żeromski Street, they noticed smashed shop windows. Some began to loot the shops. This description of events is of necessity simplified. I am not simplifying, however, when I say that from about 5 p.m. the authorities began their preparations for revenge.

Twenty years before the Radom strike, the then Premier, Józef Cyrankiewicz, said when assessing the Poznań revolt: "The hand, raised against the people's government, will be cut off". It was cut off, too, in the Baltic Coast cities in December 1970, and in Radom and Ursus in June 1976.

On 25 June, sentence was passed on the town of Radom. First came pacification, then intensive propaganda. People were treated like game in a hunt. All our Radom interlocutors have stressed the atmosphere of fear and terror. Police patrols detained incidental passers-by. People were sacked on the basis of the first pretext that came to mind, with no formalities. I read a highly curious explanation of why a worker was disciplinary dismissed: "For his negative social stance on 25 June". This was the atmosphere in which, on 30 June, a mass rally was organized in support of the policies of the Polish United Workers' Party. A subsequent act of provocation was provided by a parade of the victorious police divisions on Police Day.

The number held in the first days after the events can be estimated at several (at least two) thousand. Of these, some 200 people were chosen to stand trial. At the same time preparations for the "grand trials" were under way. Police rounded up the "main" suspects — 25 of them. We do not know who selected those formally to be indicted, and when, but while in the majority of the earlier trials it is difficult to establish the criterion for the choice of defendants, the trials whose finale took place in the Supreme Court reveal thorough stage-management. Without it, selection of those designated to play "major" roles from a crowd of several thousand outside the Party headquarters and several hundred inside the building would have been very difficult. The police had arrested all the identified participants of the demonstration, including incidental bystanders. If the detainees had a "suitable" curriculum vitae in the police files, they would become defendants. Police officers recalled criminals they knew and had seen at the demonstration. They arrested them at home and at work, occasionally a few weeks after the event. Their presence was necessary at the trials, to prove the criminal nature of the workers' protest.

Almost all the accused workers were charged with participating in the demonstration or with ransacking the Party Regional headquarters. The latter was treated like a sanctuary by the police officers, the prosecution and the judges. "The defendants committed a profanity", the police testified. The list of damages contains no mention of the Party building. The indictments refer to acts of destroying, demolishing and setting fire to an enigmatic "building of public utility". Only the court cases themselves finally revealed the name of this mysterious shrine.

Virtually none of the defendants pleaded guilty to the crimes they were accused of. This fact was of no significance; on the contrary, it was treated as an aggravating circumstance. "...A cunning criminal... trying to defend himself..." — those were the comments made by the prosecutor and judge. Admission of guilt was an aggravating circumstance too: "The defendant himself was quite unabashed when describing his participation...". During investigation, police officers made threats that should the defendant not admit his guilt, they would kill him and take his body out in a plastic sack (similar sacks were described by witnesses of the December 1970 events). In the trials themselves, the beaten and maltreated defendants were a gruesome sight.

Only a few tried actively to defend themselves. The trials were a mere confirmation of sentences decided earlier. At one of the trials, before the prosecutor had made his winding-up speech, a policeman came up to the tearful wives of the accused and said — to the wife and sister of Mr. Chomicki — "Keep your tears for nine years", and to Mrs. Gniadek, "and you, for ten". Those were indeed the sentences passed by the court later. Legal means of defence ceased to exist for those arrested after 25 June. Some of them wrote complaints and pleading letters asking for justice. Their families did the same. The complaints have remained unanswered to this day; the Public Prosecutor's Department and the police are trying to force their authors to retract, by means of threats — that the prisoners' situation will be worsened — and promises — of help, if the charges are withdrawn.

In the first phase of the reprisals, considerable success was achieved by the accompanying propaganda campaign. People in Radom believed that everything was the fault of the demonstrators. Those who were released from prison earliest, after a month, encountered social ostracism. "It's all your fault," people accused them. "Why did you steal, why did you protest...?" Participation in a strike or in the demonstration was something to be ashamed of. A man dismissed from work would be alone. In general he would not know the addresses, or even the surnames, in many cases, of his work-mates. Those sacked were forbidden to enter their factory. Inside the plants, all conversations on the subject of the events were reported by informers, and groups of people who gathered to discuss the issue would be dispersed. In such a situation, action of help and defence had to come from outside. At first, it concerned itself only with those in prison; through their families, it later reached those already released, and finally those who were sacked. The circle of people receiving aid widened. People gave the names of cell-mates, or sacked work-mates. Some actively joined the aid programme, searching for addresses, conducting conversations and handing over money. After a few weeks of this activity Radom ceased to believe in the legitimacy of the principle of collective responsibility.

Now that the programme of help for the workers can be assessed from a certain perspective, it can be stated that it has not been an act of charity. The anonymity which generally accompanies philanthropy was avoided. Bonds between people were established. At the same time it was not a political action of the International Labour Organization type, defending people with similar ideologies. The help was given not to a mythical working class but to specific, living people.

The authorities replied to the activity initiated by the Workers' Defence Committee with a programme of intimidation, which escalated after the victimized workers submitted collective complaints. The success of the police and the prosecution department was minimal: less than 20 withdrawn charges have been confirmed. This is a small figure if we consider that it took place after one of the greatest acts of terror in Poland's post-war history. A fact which should also be emphasised is that not one of the women who signed the collective complaint about the treatment of their husbands and relatives by the police and the courts withdrew her signature.

The support given to the workers aroused a feeling of solidarity. I consider this to be the second great achievement (the first being the prevention of dire poverty in a large number of families) of the activity initiated by the Workers' Defence Committee.

Jan Lityński

RESPONSE OF THE INTELLECTUALS

Within a few days after the strikes of 25 June leading Polish intellectuals came out in support of the workers. Some of their declarations are reprinted here in full. The first of these, a letter to the Polish Parliament, is sometimes mistakenly referred to as the "Letter of the 11".

A declaration of solidarity with the workers by the 14

The decision to raise food prices, massive strikes and demonstrations by the workers which were thereby provoked, then a reversal of the decision within 24 hours are facts which exposed in a dramatic way a malady in the life of our society.

The government's sagacity in being able to correct its standpoint deserves our great appreciation. As a result it was possible to avoid a repetition of the tragic events of 1956 in Poznań and of 1970 on the Coast.

We declare our solidarity with the workers of Poland. It is a sense of responsibility for the fate of the Nation and of the State which requires us to recognize the gravity of the situation. The events of the last few days have proved that in the system of government presently prevailing the only form in which the real attitudes of the people can find expression are outbursts of social discontent, outbursts which are dangerous in their consequences. Such a system cannot be continued without risk of incalculable catastrophes.

The President of the Council of Ministers promised a penetrating examination of proposals and comments on the price structuring and a reassessment of the issues. We consider that the debate cannot be resolved in the confines of government offices. It is not possible to hold this dialogue in conditions of reprisals which are seen by some as a means of rebuilding undetermined authority. For a genuine national debate to take place it is necessary to extend democratic freedoms in an essential way. On the agendum is the establishment of a real representation of the workers; without it nowadays it is not possible to study effectively the needs and aspirations of our society. In their present form the trade unions do not fulfil this role. Recent events have once again confirmed how completely fictitious the unions are. It is also impossible to envisage any kind of serious and effective public discussion in the absence of an independent press. Public opinion cannot freely take shape and find expression unless freedom of association is guaranteed.

A few months ago, during the discussion of the changes to the Constitution, such demands were voiced in many letters, memoranda and personal representations. These views were not published, their authors were variously harassed, and recently a campaign of reprisals against them has been mounted. The course of events quickly and distinctly showed how necessary it was to implement the changes demanded in the debate on the Constitution.

No one should treat these necessary reforms as unilateral concessions on the part of the government. In the difficult situation of our existence as a self-governing State they are the expression of the Nation's common interest. They are the only guarantee that issues basic to our life as a Nation shall be decided upon by ourselves.

This places upon everyone an absolute duty of both civil activeness and increased responsibility for words and deeds.

Ludwik Cohn, Jakub Karpiński, Stefan Kisielewski, Jacek Kuroń, Edward Lipiński, Rev. Stanisław Małkowski, Adam Michnik, Jan Olszewski, Józef Rybicki, Władysław Siła-Nowicki, Aniela Steinsbergowa, Adam Szczypiorski, Wacław Zawadzki, Rev. Jan Zieja.

29 June 1976

The above are all signatories of the "Letter of the 59" protesting against changes to the Constitution of the Polish People's Republic.

Kuroń's appeal to the Italian Communist leader, Berlinguer

I am turning to you as a leader of a Workers' party, as a politician who fights for a socialism that is consistent with human rights, as a communist, because my country is ruled indivisibly by communists.

I appeal for your help for Polish workers who are being denigrated by the press, radio and television, who are being beaten up by the militia, who have been arrested, who stand in court accused of sabotage and are convicted to long sentences of loss of freedom.

As you doubtlessly know, on 24 June, Piotr Jaroszewicz, Premier of the Polish People's Republic and a member both of the Political Bureau and of the Secretariat of the Central Committee of the PZPR [Polish United Workers' Party], put forward plans of a general price-increase on food articles. According to these plans the new prices of many articles represented an increase of about 100%. As a result of the price and pay structure in Poland this meant to a large proportion of worker families a lowering of living standards beyond the minimum of necessity.

Discussion in Parliament was limited to a statement by Edward Babiuch, Member of Parliament, who is also a member of the Political Bureau and of the Central Committee of the PZPR. Speaking for all the parliamentary clubs and groupings, Babiuch supported the government plans and announced the intention of consulting with the workers. Less than 48 hours were reserved for these consultations. This is sufficient evidence of the fictitious character of the consultation that had been announced.

In these circumstances the workers reacted spontaneously by an almost general break-off from work and by holding street demonstrations in many localities. During these demonstrations, on 25 June at about 9 a.m., workers of the Ursus farm-tractor factory on the outskirts of Warsaw occupied the Warsaw to Łódź and the Warsaw to Poznań railway lines disrupting rail services. In the afternoon they dismantled the rails and one locomotive was derailed.

In Radom there was an encounter between workers and special police squads, lasting several hours. During the encounter the regional Party headquarters was set on fire and barricades were put up in streets.

Under the pressure of the workers' demonstration the authorities backed out of their plan of price increases — 24 hours after their announcement. The communiqué of the PZPR Political Bureau regarding changes to the planned price increases, published on 14 July, concedes the point to the demonstrators.

The June events are symptomatic of a grave malady in the life of our society. Complete responsibility for this state of affairs rests with the authorities, who deprived the working class and the whole society of altogether all means of expression for their views and of defending their own interests.

History is repeating itself yet a third time. In October 56 in Poznań and in December '70 on our Baltic Coast, Polish workers paid with their own blood for the mistakes of those in power. No conclusions were drawn from these experiences. This time, too, nothing is said about the authorities' responsibility; far from it, instead, reprisals directed at the workers are the sole response.

Criminal offences should be punished, but it is intolerable that demonstrators should be punished for resisting the militia, when those who perpetrated the bloody massacre of the workers on our Baltic coast [in 1970] escaped all punishment. Relegation of moral and legal responsibility to the participants of the workers' demonstrations for damages done, when it was not in their power to organize properly the demonstrations, has nothing to do with lawfulness. This is a

73

case of vengeance exacted by people who during thirty years of rule learnt nothing and understood nothing.

In the press, on radio and television, the demonstrations which forced the state authorities to change their misconceived views, are described as the work of hooligans, as acts of brigandism and vandalism. In many areas massive reprisals are being applied to the participants of the demonstrations and strikes. Since the demonstrations were of a spontaneous character the authorities and the militia lost control over the situation and reprisals are now often directed at people who were present only by chance at places where the incidents occurred. Workers are being sacked everywhere; in Radom and at the Ursus factory many have been arrested; those who have returned from the police stations bear the signs of beating that at times was very severe.

On 16 and 17 July trials were held in Warsaw of seven workers from Ursus, charged with sabotage (art. 220 of the Polish Criminal Code). According to the indictment the sabotage consisted of the derailing of a locomotive weighing 40 tons by a group of people. The accused were not allowed to see their families, each of them was arbitrarily assigned an official defence counsel. Except for nominated persons, neither the public nor journalists were allowed to attend the trial, though formally it was not held behind closed doors. Liability of the accused is proved solely on the basis of photographs taken by the militia. One of the accused twice tried to tell the court that he had been beaten during investigation, but the presiding judge did not allow the statement to be made.

This is the first trial connected with the June incidents in Warsaw. But there are many workers in prison suspected of similar acts.

Not having their own organizations and deprived of information, the workers are completely defenceless in the face of reprisals. The response of the authorities exacerbates the feelings of hatred and desperation. The next outburst may cause tragedy for the Polish Nation and may mean political bankruptcy of the Left in the whole of Europe.

With regard to smaller localities, we have absolutely no possiblity of surveilling the methods of police inquiry or of the courts which are completely dependent on the political authorities.

Only total amnesty for all participants of the June demonstrations can put an end to the anti-worker intimidation. Public opinion in countries where it is truly free, can take up the fight for amnesty.

I know that Western Europe sets great store by your opinions, as do also the authorities in Poland.

I appeal to your conscience. May it not prove indifferent to this cause.

11 July 1976 [Published in Unità, 20 July 1976]

Open letter from J. Andrzejewski

"To the persecuted participants of the workers' protest"

Being deeply concerned and embittered by the wrongs and injustices which you are suffering and as each day brings fresh confirmation from all quarters that many of my friends, many writers, and the Polish progressive-thinking intelligentsia in the main, share my thoughts and feelings, I wish to extend to you in these your difficult days expressions of respect and solidarity and to send words of hope and encouragement.

I realize that in the face of court verdicts which sentence you to many years of imprisonment, in the face of violence and physical oppression to which you were subjected and amidst feelings of helplessness which are your daily bread and which are the heaviest of defeats to suffer in all of human degradation, and in the face of your imperilled material existence resulting from the mass dismissals from work that fall to your lot each day, my words are just words and their gravity is incommensurably slight in comparison with your sufferings.

They are, however, the only means by which I may express my association with you, my sympathy and my protest.

I wish you to know, at a time when the authorities use the press, radio and television in an attempt to mislead public opinion and to turn its attention away from the real reasons for the crisis that has arisen, by making allegations against you of socially damaging activity, of destructive anarchy or even of hooliganism — that there are people in Poland who are immune to deception and hypocrisy and have preserved their ability to discern truth from falsehood and who see in you, the persecuted workers, not only spokesmen for an immediate and specific cause, but, above all, fighters for true socialist

75

democracy and for social liberty without which all freedom perishes and deceitful clichés reign over public life, the nation is in danger and the life of individuals is stifled.

The thoughts and hearts of these people go out to you. All progressive Europe and the world looks on anxiously to see whether the Polish authorities will dare to throw off their responsibility for the crisis onto those who warned against the consequences of erroneous decisions and who by their protests prevented their immediate implementation.

I wish to promise you personally and also on behalf of my circle of friends, Polish writers, who have taken up your cause with several distinguished figures representing the world of culture and politics in Europe, that we shall not cease in our endeavours to secure an end to the persecutions to which you have fallen victims and which you still risk.

We demand amnesty for those who have been unjustly convicted and imprisoned, the freeing of those who have been arrested without cause, the rehabilitation of those whose reputation has been damaged and denigrated, the reinstatement to employment of those who have been deprived of it. As long as even one of you, the participants of the workers' protest, remains in danger of being exposed to violence or physical oppression, of being forcibly separated from his family or from society, of being harassed at his place of work or in civic life, we shall use all the means available to us, albeit unfortunately very limited, to stand up for you.

Poland is not only our common Motherland, but also our common possession. Let us defend her!

Jerzy Andrzejewski

28 July 1976

The appeal of the 13

On 20 July 1976 the Warsaw District Court sentenced to various terms of imprisonment (up to five years) seven participants in the workers' demonstrations which took place on 25 June in the tractor-producing plant "Ursus", near Warsaw. The purpose of this mass-demonstration, one of the most impressive to have taken place in Poland, was to protest against drastic price increases. The trial was conducted under conditions which violated the principle of openness of judicial proceedings. Only the close relatives of the accused were permitted to be present; entry to the court-room was totally prohibited to the foreign journalists, numerous intellectuals and students who wished to attend. The accused workers were charged with "active participation in acts of hooliganism". There were only officially-nominated defence counsel.

At the same time another trial took place in Radom. The participants in the mass demonstration there were sentenced to terms of up to 10 years in prison. And the Polish press has announced that further trials are to take place.

We consider it our duty to denounce the official condemnation describing as "acts of hooliganism" the workers' protest against unjust social policy and the government's authoritarian methods. It is necessary to state emphatically that the responsibility for the violation of law during the events in Ursus and other places, rests with the authorities, who have abolished the elementary forms of workers' democracy, have destroyed the "workers' councils" created in 1956, and have reduced the trade unions to a fictitious, dead organization completely subordinated to the ruling apparatus. In order to avoid a repetition of such dramatic events in the future, it is imperative to restore to the workers rights which are properly theirs, and not to resort to repression.

The political struggle of the Polish people for these rights, previously manifested in the numerous protests against the recent changes in the Constitution, is a struggle for democratic socialism, a socialism defined by Karl Marx as "the very opposite of the situation where man is humiliated, an abandoned slave held in contempt".

We are only too aware that Polish public opinion cannot hear our voices through normal channels, but we are convinced that we express the feelings of the majority of the population. That is why we are addressing ourselves through your journal to all those who are fighting for workers' rights which are an integral part of human rights.

We are making the following appeal: help the imprisoned Polish workers! The information reaching us from prisons and court-rooms demonstrates that the security police are using methods of physical violence during the interrogations. Moreover, it is generally known that the workers suspected of having taken part in the demonstrations are sacked *en masse* from their jobs; such dismissals endanger their own and their families' material existence.

We appeal to: Jean-Paul Sartre, André Malraux, Pierre Emmanuel, Louis Aragon, Jean-Marie Domenach, Claude Roy, Jean Daniel.

We also appeal to: Gunther Grass, Heinrich Böll, Arthur Miller, Saul Bellow, Eugenio Montale, Ignazio Silone, Stephen Spender and Robert Conquest.

We appeal to all who feel solidarity with the struggle of the workers the world over, for the liberation of labour: Demand the release of the imprisoned Polish workers!

Stanisław Barańczak, poet; Jacek Bocheński, writer; Kazimierz Brandys, writer; Stefan Kisielewski, journalist and writer; Andrzej Kijowski, journalist and writer; Ryszard Krynicki, economist; Jan Józef Lipski, literary critic and historian; Adam Michnik, historian; Halina Mikołajska, actress; Marek Nowakowski, writer; Julian Stryjowski, writer; Rev. Jan Zieja; Edward Lipiński, economist.

[*Liberation* (Paris), 28 July 1976]

Chapter five

THE WORKERS' DEFENCE COMMITTEE

In September 1976, fifteen prominent intellectuals organized them-selves into a committee which has come to be known as the Workers' Defence Committee (the WDC), and which would act in the open. They set out their aims in the following words:

"... to provide legal, financial, and medical aid for the victims of reprisals. Since the trade unions, the social welfare agencies and official bodies whose duties should include the defence of workers' interests, are unable or unwilling to do so, a voluntary group has had to take over their responsibilities."

The WDC collected detailed information about reprisals particularly in Radom and Warsaw where the behaviour of the authorities was especially brutal; it has given substantial financial assistance to hundreds of families in distress (cf. p. 86–87); it has helped with legal costs; its members have regularly attended court hearings. The WDC has published communiqués about its work, which are circulated in samizdat form. These com-muniqués and the press conferences held by members of the Committee have revealed to the outside world the nature and scale of the authorities' actions.

As a group dedicated to protect workers the WDC itself has no political aims. Its deliberate policy of working openly, despite harass-ment by the authorities, ensures that its members cannot be accused of belonging to a clandestine organization. But, that the protection of workers is necessary in a system, where constitutionally, power belongs to the rural and urban working people, makes the grouping all the more unique. Its practical objectives, its pressing tasks, have caused it to become a centre of mass "opposition" uniting all social classes; for, it is eagerly helped by many sections of the community — students who continually deliver allowances to the families of victimized workers, priests who organize collections in their parishes and lawyers with ex-perience in political trials who have managed to win a number of appeals. It has even received the indirect support of the Church.

Members of the WDC are pledged to end their work only when the last worker is released from jail for taking part in the June events, when all those who have been unjustly treated receive fair compensation and when a Parliamentary Commission is established to inquire into all aspects of the June events including the behaviour of the police. This last demand has been taken up in petitions to the authorities by an unprecedented number of luminaries of society.

Since the Committee's work is a constant reminder of the excesses of the régime, the authorities would certainly like to stop it from functioning. Moreover, its publicized contacts with other dissidents in Soviet-bloc countries such as with Sakharov and the signatories of "Charter 77" in Czechoslovakia, present the Communist leadership with the worrying problem that a permanent liaison between the various national dissidents may develop into a broader base of opposition. On the other hand, the strictly humanitarian character of its action, the support it commands in Poland and the publicity and backing which it has gained in the West, makes it a very difficult body to crush. The recent arrests of some of its younger, more dynamic members, as well as a number of its active supporters, have been widely criticized in the West.

What promise can the unpredictable future hold for such movements within society itself? One hope is that the Party might base itself upon this force within society and identify with some limited fragment of the nation's aspirations for freedom (as is argued in the texts of Chapter seven. Nevertheless the limits of opposition in any totalitarian state are very narrow and the WDC has stepped well beyond them. This serves as an example of what individuals committed to a belief in basic human rights can do. Thus, whatever the cost may prove to be, the process of organized opposition has been set in motion in Poland and, what is all the more important for the future, large numbers of young people have been actively involved.

Below is reproduced a document announcing the Committee's formation. This is followed by Communiqué No. 4, chosen on account of its comprehensive coverage of the Committee's work, and is further supplemented by extracts from later communiqués, while a "digest" tabulates the growing scope of the WDC's information and disbursements. The communiqués all bear the signatures and addresses of committee members, the number of which rose from the original 15 to 25, and these are listed separately on p. 83–85.

From: Jerzy Andrzejewski,
Warsaw, 23rd September 1976.

To the President of the Sejm
of the Polish People's Republic

Rt. Honourable Sir,

On behalf of the Committee for the Defence of Workers Victimized as a Result of the Events of 25th June 1976, I take the liberty of submitting to you, for the information of the Sejm and the governing authorities of the Polish People's

Republic, an appeal by the Committee, simultaneously announcing by this means the fact of its formation. Our appeal includes proposals for an amnesty, which we wish to direct first and foremost to the Sejm.

Respectfully yours,
Jerzy Andrzejewski,
Member of the Committee.

Warsaw, September 1976

An Appeal to the People and the Government of Poland

The workers' protests against the excessive price increases, expressing as it did the attitude of virtually the whole population, was followed by brutal repression. Demonstrators in Ursus, Radom and other towns were arrested in great numbers, beaten and kicked. The most widespread of the measures taken was dismissal from work, which, apart from the arrests themselves, has been especially severe in its consequence for the families of the victimized workers.

The repressions as a rule involved a breach of the law on the part of the authorities. Courts gave verdicts without evidence; people were thrown out of work in defiance of the Work Code. The authorities did not refrain from obtaining confessions by force. Such conduct is, unfortunately, by no means new to us. We need only recall the unlawful repressive measures taken against the signatories of letters protesting about changes in the Constitution: some were expelled from their place of work or college, unlawfully interrogated, blackmailed. Not for a long time, however, have repressive measures been so violent and on such a large scale as at present. It is the first time for many years that arrests and interrogations have been accompanied by physical terror.

The victims of the current bout of repressions cannot hope to obtain aid and protection from the institutions formed to provide them, e.g. from the Trade Unions, which play a pitiful role. Social security departments are also refusing to help. In this situation the task must be taken over by the community at large, in whose interests the victimized workers came out, since our society has no means of defending itself against unlawfulness other than by solidarity and mutual help.

It is for this reason that the undersigned have formed a

Workers' Defence Committee with the purpose of initiating all forms of defence and help. Financial, medical and legal aid is essential. Full information concerning the victimization is no less important. It is our conviction that only the public exposure of the conduct of the authorities can provide an effective means of defence. For this reason we ask, among other things, that all who have been subjected to victimization or know of such cases, pass on the relevant information to Members of the Committee.

According to the Committee's information 160,000 zlotys has been collected to date and used for the purpose of aid. The needs, however, are much greater; they can only be catered for by the initiative of society as a whole. Wherever in our country there are victims of repression, it is the duty of society to rally to their defence. In every community, every factory or institution there must be brave people willing to initiate collective means of help and assistance.

The repressive measures used against the workers constitute a violation of fundamental human rights, recognized both in international law and in Polish legislature: the right to work, to strike, the right freely to express one's convictions, the right to participate in meetings and demonstrations. For this reason the Committee, concurring with the Resolution of the Conference of the Episcopate of Poland of 9th September 1976, calls for an amnesty for those convicted and arrested and demands that all who have been subjected to repressions be allowed to return to work.

The Committee calls on the people to support these demands.

It is our deepest conviction that by bringing the Workers' Defence Committee to life and to activity we are fulfilling our human and patriotic duty, serving the good cause of the Motherland, the Nation, and Man.

Committee for the Defence of Workers,
Victimized as a Result of the Events
of 25th June 1976.

Jerzy Andrzejewski, Stanisław Barańczak, Ludwik Cohn, Jacek Kuroń, Edward Lipiński, Jan Józef Lipski, Antoni Macierewicz, Piotr Naimski, Antoni Pajdak, Józef Rybicki, Aniela Steinsbergowa, Adam Szczypiorski, Rev. Jan Zieja, Wojciech Ziembiński.

Members of the Workers' Defence Committee as at June 1977

1. Jerzy ANDRZEJEWSKI — writer, State Award Winner, Warsaw, Świerczewskiego 53 Flat 4, tel. 19 82 61.

2. Stanisław BARAŃCZAK — poet and literary theorist, Research Fellow at Poznań, Kościuszki 110 Flat 9, tel. 55 441.

3. Bogdan BORUSEWICZ — historian, Lublin Catholic University graduate, imprisoned as a grammar school student for his part in the March 1968 events, Sopot, 23 March 96 Flat 24.

4. Mirosław CHOJECKI — chemist, member of the Students' Democratic Movement in 1968, Polish Scouting Movement activist, Warsaw, Sarbiewskiego 2 Flat 47, tel. 35 25 37.

5. Ludwik COHN — barrister-at-law, Polish Socialist Party activist in the inter-war period, defender of Warsaw in 1920 and 1939 campaigns, POW in Germany, political prisoner of the stalinist period, Warsaw, Koszykowa 14 Flat 6, tel. 27 51 64.

6. Stefan KACZOROWSKI — former Secretary General of the Christian Democratic Party, former Chairman, Warsaw Council of the Work Party during the occupation, fought in the Warsaw Uprising, publicist, founder-member of the *Odrodzenie* literary circle.

7. Anka KOWALSKA — writer, withdrew from PAX [pro-communist "catholic" grouping] in 1968, prize-winner of the Pietrzak Award [a PAX literary award], Warsaw, Estońska 4, tel. 17 53 07.

8. Jacek KUROŃ — teacher, political prisoner in 1965–71, Warsaw, Mickiewicza 27 Flat 64, tel. 39 39 64.

9. Professor Edward LIPIŃSKI — economist, Member of the Polish Academy of Sciences, State Award Winner, former Polish Socialist Party executive, Warsaw, Rakowiecka 22a Flat 26, tel. 54 58 17.

10. Jan Józef LIPSKI — literary critic and historian, veteran of the underground A.K. (Home Army) and of the Warsaw Uprising, former Chairman of the *Crooked Circle Club* (1956–7), Warsaw, Konopczyńskiego 4 Flat 9, tel. 27 34 72.

11. Antoni MACIEREWICZ — historian, member of the Student Democratic Movement in 1968 and of the Polish Scouting Movement, Warsaw, Pańska 61 Flat 125.

12. Adam MICHNIK — historian, political prisoner in 1968–69, private secretary to writer Antoni Słonimski, visted the West late '76 to '77, author of "The Church — The Left Dialogue", Warsaw, Al. Przyjaciół 9 m. 3, tel. 28 43 55.

13. Halina MIKOŁAJSKA — actress, twice State Award Winner, Warsaw, Marszałkowska 10/16, tel. 21 54 37.

14. Emil MORGIEWICZ — lawyer, political prisoner 1970–74, member of Amnesty International, Warsaw, Agnieszki 4.

15. Piotr NAIMSKI — biochemist, Polish Scouting Movement instructor, Pańska 61 Flat 125 c/o A. Macierewicz.

16. Wojciech ONYSZKIEWICZ — historian, member of the Student Democratic Movement in 1968.

17. Antoni PAJDAK — barrister-at-law, former Polish Socialist Party Activist, veteran of First World War Polish Legion and of Socialist Movement under Nazi occupation, wartime Deputy Delegate of the Polish Government in Exile, tried and sentenced by a Moscow court in the trial of 16 Polish leaders in 1945, prisoner in USSR in 1945–56, Warsaw, Śliska 10 Flat 76.

18. Józef RYBICKI — Ph.D., former Headmaster, a campaigner against alcoholism, former Commander of the A.K. (Home Army) Special Unit "Kedyw" for the Warsaw Region under Nazi occupation, veteran of the Warsaw Uprising, Knight of the Virtuti Militari Cross, for many years political prisoner in the stalinist period, Milanówek, Okólna 14a, tel. 58 35 51.

19. Aniela STEINSBERGOWA — barrister-at-law, pre-war defence counsel in political trials (e.g. in the trial of strike leaders at "Semperit" works in Cracow), former member of the Polish Socialist Party, defence counsel in post-war political trials (e.g. rehabilitation trials of members of the A.K.), Warsaw, Boya Żeleńskiego 4, Flat 26, tel. 25 32 93.

20. Professor Adam SZCZYPIORSKI — historian, former Polish Socialist Party activist, Warsaw, Parkowa 13/17, tel. 41 24 72.

21. Józef ŚRENIOWSKI — ethnographer and sociologist, member of the Student Democratic Movement in 1968, political prisoner in 1968, Łódź, Laurowa 2.

22. Rev. Jan ZIEJA — Polish Army Chaplain in the 1920 and 1939 campaigns, Knight of the Virtuti Militari Cross, chaplain of the Underground Scouting Movement "Szare Szeregi" A.K. (Home Army) and of the "Baszta" A.K. (Home Army) Regiment, veteran of the Warsaw Uprising, Warsaw, Dobra 59 Flat 13.

23. Wacław ZAWADZKI — writer, former Polish Socialist Party member, former Chairman of the "Wiedza" Publishing Co-operative, Warsaw, Stołeczna 3, tel. 33 23 92.

24. Wojciech ZIEMBIŃSKI — editor, painter and designer, veteran of the A.K. (Home Army) and of the Polish Armed Forces in the West, prisoner of the Gestapo in France (1942–43) and of concentration camps in Germany, Warsaw, Sady Żoliborskie 7a Flat 21, tel. 33 05 46.

Note: Ziembiński resigned from the WDC on 23 July 1977 in view of greater commitments to the "Human and Civil Rights Movement in Poland". Two new members were announced in July:
Rev. Dr. Zbigniew Kamiński — former academic chaplain and chaplain of the A.K.
Prof. Dr. Jan Kielanowski — Member of the Polish Academy of Sciences and of the German Academy, holder of an honorary doctorate from Berlin and Edinburgh, ex-director of the Institute of Animal Husbandry, former soldier of the A.K.

DIGEST OF INFORMATION: Identified Cases of Reprisal and WDC Disbursements

1. URSUS & WARSAW

Information contained in Communiques No. 1 – 7 & 11

Date of Communiqué	29 Sept. 76	10 Oct.	30 Oct.	22 Nov.	21 Dec.	15 Jan. 77	5 Feb.	30 June
No. cases identified	126	144 (258 according to hearsay)	208	209	220	226	252 125 in direct contact	202 from Ursus + 6 in Warsaw + 169 in direct contact
No. Families receiving support	67	89	100	107	109	115	153	
No. known to be in custody	13	3 incl.Majewski hospitalized with multiple jaw-fractures	3	3		3 tried for dismantling rails		
No. sentenced by tribunals by courts	59 19	60 to 3 mths 21 (16 suspended sentences)	50 21				125	
Remarks	Charges of larceny were made	15 cases of release after 48 hr arrest 8 released pending inquiries re: dismantling of rails		24 appeals for reinstatement Only 4 successful				The raided eggs p. 53 officially now valued at 155,000 zl.despite Court estimate of 80,000 zl.
No. dismissals from work			167		109			
No. re-employed but elsewhere	10	10	29	54			71	
No. reinstated	2	4	15	15		19	19	
Aid (cummulative) in Zlotys	139,200	205,600	258,000	338,170	484,510	554,900	644,550	715,470
Emergency payments		37,470	37,470	39,900	301,800			
Regular support	51,000 monty	65,000 monthly	140,440	198,160	172,710			
Legal aid			80,290	100,110				
Legal debts		134,000	114,800	137,140	33,020		26,300	

DIGEST OF INFORMATION: Identified Cases of Reprisals and WDC Disbursements

2. RADOM

Information based on Communiqués No. 1 – 7 & 11

Date of Communiqué	29 Sept. 76	10 Oct.	30 Oct.	22 Nov.	21 Dec.	15 Jan. 77	16 Feb.	30 June
No. Cases identified of the 2000 estimated*	70	114	150	292	394 294 in direct contact	423 301 in direct contact	493	511
No. of families receiving support	30	53	71	85 (legal aid to 34)	45 + legal aid to 63 + medical aid to 15		115 (legal aid: 86 medical aid: 21)	274 (legal aid: 92 medical aid:39)
No. tried charges sentences	13 by tribunals 44 by courts larceny assault on police	75 known 44 sentenced to over 2 yrs	131 known 48 over 2 yrs 11 3 mths–2yrs 39 less than 3 mths	261 known 52 over 2 yrs 37 3 mths–2yrs 48 less than 3 mths	202 jailed 74 over 2 yrs 56 3 mths–2 yrs 72 less than 3 mths		261	
Extreme cases	Dead: Rev. Brozyna 3 more said to be killed	4 known cases of death, more said to be dead 7 hospitalized	Dead: Rev. Kotlarz Brozyna Lamecki Zabecki 9 hospitalised					
Financial aid in zlotys	20,800 mainly legal	72,300	105,300 + legal costs of 430,000	304,960	494,650	794,300	1,076,700	1,663,560

Note. By 22 July 1977 all prisoners were free. However, "Those who were re-employed over the past months (with only a few exceptions) continue to work under substantially worse conditions than prior to the strike." ((WDC Communiqué No 13, 31 Aug. 1977)

* Estimate based on size of prisons known to be involved

WORKERS' DEFENCE COMMITTEE

Warsaw 22nd November, 1976

Communiqué No. 4

All the reports in the Communiqué refer to cases examined by the Committee. This document brings up to date information contained in the Communiqués Nos 1, 2 and 3 of the 29.9, 10.1 and 30.10.1976 respectively. The figures for reprisals following the June events have yet to be made public and it remains difficult to assess the totals involved. Whenever we have to refer to unchecked information we shall give our sources or reasons which lead us to accept it.

1. Number of Detainees and Prisoners

According to our estimates, at least 2,000 people were originally detained in Radom and 500 in Ursus. We have been able to identify so far 261 persons sentenced either by a court or a special tribunal in Radom and 112 in Ursus. We are unable to give figures for the number detained at present since some are released while their appeals are pending and others, previously released, have been re-arrested. We have, however, firm information on three people still detained without trial in Ursus.

2. Radom Trials

Four major trials took place during July and August. The accused were charged with hooliganism, assaulting personnel on duty, injuring 75 policemen and deliberately damaging public property to the value of more than 28 million zlotys. The charges were under article 275 of the criminal code. During the disturbances an attempt had been made to set fire to the Radom Party headquarters, but the building has not been included in the list of 25 damaged properties submitted in evidence by the public prosecutor despite the fact that certain of the accused were found guilty of arson in connection with the fire.

The following were sentenced in Radom: —

1. On 16–17 July (Case No II DS 38/76) Henryk Bednarczyk — 4 years, Stanisław Gorka — 5 years, Ryszard Grudzień — 9 years, Tadeusz Mitak — 8 years, Wojciech Mitak — 6 years, Zygmunt Zaborowski — 10 years.

2. On 26–27 July (Case No II DS 40/76) Antoni Maria Dyg-
nas — 5 years, Wiesław Kobyłko — 8 years, Stanisław
Kowalski — 3 years, Edward Sawicki — 5 years, Wiesław
Skrzypek — 9 years, Henryk Szczęsny — 5 years.

3. On 3–5 August (Case No II DS 16/76) Czesław Chomicki — 9 years, Wiesław Długosz — 9 years, Andrzej
Bogdan Filipowski — 3 years, Krzysztof Gniadek — 10
years, Waldemar Gutowski — 4 years, Marian Janicki
— 5 years.

A notice of appeal has been given by the defence in all
three cases. The first appeal is to be heard on 10 December.
Only the first of the three trials has been mentioned in the
national press. The second has been reported only in the local
paper and the third has not been reported at all.

Besides the group trials, at least a hundred individual
cases have been tried on similar charges under article 275.
The sentences varied from a few months to 3 years; in some
cases, suspended sentences have been given. A number of
prisoners, tried under articles 236 and 234 of the criminal code,
were charged with assault and insulting behaviour towards
the police and members of other security bodies. The Committee has been able to record 11 cases of this kind. It is
estimated that 100 or so people were charged with theft. The
committee has identified 21 such cases. The hearings in Radom
continue, but we have not been able to build up a complete
documentation of current cases. After a hearing lasting from
October 28th to November 17th, the following were found
guilty and sentenced: Krzysztof Sulek (Article 236) — 6 months,
Marian Jastrzębski (Article 208) — 2 years and a fine, Marian
Noga (Article 234) — a suspended sentence of 1 year, Krzysztof Szerling (Article 236) — a fine of 7,000 zlotys, Piotr Wójcik
(Articles 275 and 208) — suspended 2 years sentence and 5,000
zlotys fine, Stanisław Winiarski (Article 236) — sentence unknown. The trial of Józef Smagowski (Article 275) was removed to another court.

The following defendants and witnesses: M. Jastrzębski,
B. Cieśliński and A. B. Filipowski, made statements to the
effect that they have been beaten during examination so as
to induce them to make false confessions.

A number of people were present in court during the trials without being in any way harassed by the police. They were: Wojciech Arkuszewski, Krzysztof Babiński, Mirosław Chojecki, Andrzej Drawicz, Jerzy Jurkiewicz, Anna Kowalska, Halina Mikołajska, Adam Pomorski, Ryszard Rubinstein, Andrzej Seweryn, Eugenia Siemaszkiewicz, Barbara Toruńczyk. We shall have more news in the next communiqué about some Ursus frials as yet unreported.

3. Reprisals in other localities

We have collected information about reprisals, mainly in the form of dismissal from work, from Nowy Targ, Łódź, Gdańsk, Pruszcz Gdański, Elbląg, Płock, Szczecin, Starachowice and Warsaw. Between two and four hundred were sacked from the Lenin Shipyard in Gdańsk, about three hundred from the Starachowice heavy vehicle plant, 200 to 250 from a shoe factory in Nowy Targ. In Gdańsk we were able to identify by name ninety-two workers dismissed from various plants. Sixty-eight of the dismissed appealed to the arbitration commissions before the 31 July. Fifty three appeals were dismissed, eleven were settled out of court and three resulted in reinstatement at the various plants by the commissions. Twenty workers appealed to the labour tribunals before the 29 September. The workers were tried in accordance with the following instructions contained in a document issued by the Department of Employment and Social Welfare of the Gdańsk City Council dated 8 July "The managements are reminded that regulations concerning re-employment of workers whose contract has been severed without notice should be stringently observed". As previously in Radom and Ursus, the dismissals were in breach of the labour code. Article 52 of the code has been interpreted so as to make it into a strike breaking measure. Two typical cases were those of Edward Szreder and Józef Zapolnik. Szreder's contract has been terminated because "he enjoyed considerable authority and his action encouraged others to stop work". Józef Zapolnik was also dismissed without notice, although "on the date in question, he had been off work on a medical certificate and had only called at the shipyard to collect the funeral allowance as he had buried a daughter two days previously". (Information taken from a document signed by the Chairman of the appeal commission in Gdańsk.) Henryk Kicha of the Gdańsk shipyard was sacked because, as Chairman of the local committee of Socialist Youth, he called a meeting in defence of Jan Trzaska (previously dismissed) and tried to collect signatures for a protest petition. Mieczysław Traczyk, also from the Gdańsk shipyard has been sacked because at a general meeting of the shipyard workers, he demanded that price increases be re-examined by economists.

In a shoe factory in Nowy Targ, the workers struck in protest against false press reports. About 250 people were sacked and only 50 were reinstated.

On the 25th June, a number of plants went on strike in Łódź. We have not got a complete list of those concerned. In the Małgorzata Fornalska textile factory, the workers formed a strike committee and on 1 July approximately 300 workers were sacked on the spot, allegedly under article 52 of the labour code. Almost all are now back at work, after a period of unemployment lasting between 1 and 4 months. Generally, the employment subsequently offered is not as good as that which they had prior to the strike.

In the Fornalska works, a number of dismissed workers appealed to the labour tribunal and some of these were reinstated as a result of tribunal decisions. On the other hand, the arbitration commission invariably decided against the workers. Later in July, all the sacked workers were told to report to the police headquarters. They were questioned about their means of livelihood and were told to report to the police when they found new employment.

4. The aid for the workers of Ursus, Radom and Łódź

Ursus

We have been able to identify 209 cases. Regular support reaches 107 families. 69 of 209 people are back at work, 15 of them at the Ursus plant.

Some people left the region to look for work elsewhere. 24 appealed to the labour tribunal for re-instatement, but only four won their case.

Three people are still detained without trial. The trial of two of them has been postponed again, and the court rejected the request by the defence to release them until the hearing.

One of the accused, Marek Majewski, has spent four months in a prison hospital as a result of beatings and a fractured jaw. It transpired in court that his hospital admission card specifically stated that he had been badly injured as a result of being maltreated.

No results have been announced concerning the enquiry held by the office of the Public Prosecutor into the case of Mirosław Chmielewski, who was beaten up by the police.

The Committee have spent 338,170 zlotys in Ursus, 39,900 zlotys on emergency payments, 198,160 zlotys on regular support and 100,110 zlotys to pay some of the legal costs incurred. The legal costs outstanding amount to 137,140 zlotys. Reinstatement at work is the most crucial problem at the moment. The management of Ursus informed the Central Committee of the Party that 500 have been dismissed and only 15 reinstated so far. The Ursus workers sent a letter of protest, signed by 889 employees, to Edward Gierek.

Their demands include reinstatement of all those dismissed on the terms they enjoyed previously, without a loss of continuity of employment and with back-pay covering the period out of work. "Only then shall we be able to join with the rest of the nation to face the grave economic plight of the country" the workers' letter stated.

A copy has been sent to the management of Ursus. No reply has been received from Edward Gierek, but it is known that many workers have been threatened with dismissal unless they remove their signatures from the letter.

Radom

We have identified 292 cases of victimization. Eighty-five families have been helped financially, and legal aid has been extended to 34 people. 261 sentences have been passed, 54 of over 2 years, 37 of between 3 months and 2 years and 48 of under 3 months. 21 sentences were for larceny, 118 for taking part in mass demonstrations, assault on police and damage to property. In 122 cases we have not been able to establish either the charge or the length of sentence.

Practically all the sacked workers are back at work. In accordance with the resolution No. 68 of the Council of Ministers dated 4 April 1975, their pay has been reduced by two grades. We also know that some workers were made to renounce the back pay due to them for the period out of work in exchange for the promise of re-engagement without loss of continuity of employment.

The Committee recently received copies of a number of letters sent to the office of the Public Prosecutor with demands to bring action against persons responsible for reprisals. The complaints have been sent by Janina Brożyna (whose husband has been murdered), Danuta Chomicka (husband beaten up and sentenced to 9 years imprisonment), Zbigniew Cibor, Janina Nazimek (son beaten up and sentenced to 2 years imprisonment), Ryszard Nowak (beaten up and sentenced to 18 months in prison), Józef Szczepanik, Stanisław Wijata.

304,960 zlotys have been spent in Radom.

Łódź

Thirty-four victims of reprisals have been identified and 15,000 zlotys spent. All the 34 have now got a job of sorts, but they are still in need of help, since the period of unemployment meant great hardship for families, particularly large ones.

In Radom, Ursus and Łódź, the committee have spent 658,000 zlotys altogether. 230 families are being looked after on a regular basis. We have not succeeded in getting in touch with other families affected, even though we know about their plight. This is particularly true about Radom where we have recently been able to identify a further 133 victims of reprisals. Similarly, in Łódź, we daily receive more details about people in need of help following the reprisals. We may have to cut the size of individual monthly allowances next month to make the money go further.

5. Official Action against the Committee and its work

On November the 3rd, the security service searched the flats of two members, Jacek Kuroń and Jan Józef Lipski on a warrant from the office of the Public Prosecutor. The warrant alleged "disseminating false information". As the Workers' Defence Committee works openly and reports factually on the official reprisals against the participants of the June strikes and disturbances, a search for our communiqué and statements could hardly have been the real reason for issuing the warrant.

On November 3rd Piotr Naimski, another member of the Committee, was taken by force to Zalesie Górne where an attempt was made to take a statement from him.

Warsaw students and girl guides are taking an active part in the Aid Action. We suspect that this was the reason for the police entering twice a flat belonging to G. Jaglarska. On the first occasion (November 12th), there was a meeting of girl guide instructors. On the second occasion (November 15th), there was a party. The police detained 20 people and tried to take statements from them.

6. Forgeries

We have previously mentioned forged Communiqué No. 3, dated 25th October, 1976. A forged Communiqué No. 4, undated, and a forged "Information Bulletin" dated November 1976, are also in circulation. The Committee has never sent its Communiqués by post and does not intend to do so. We have already advised caution to people who intend to send us money. We now have to warn anyone who receives documents allegedly issued by the Committee, that, unless they are delivered by persons known to them, they may be forged.

7. Further List of Persons Active in Reprisals

Ursus. The following have been noted for their part in the campaign against the signatories of the letter of protest [p. 112] sent to the authorities: Wiesław Biernacki (head of department), Wacław Zwierz (secretary of the Party organization in the chassis shop), Jan Kraśniewski (an activist in the Party organization in the same shop), A. Świst (another local Party activist) and one Cegiełkowski.

8. Statements issued by the Committee

On 4th November, the Committee replied to an announcement by the Chief Public Prosecutor. The Committee stated that most of those arrested in Radom were charged with taking part in a political demonstration and not with looting as the Chief Public Prosecutor would have it. The Committee pointed out that the detainees have been tortured and beaten up, a fact not mentioned by the Chief Public Prosecutor.

94

On 5th November, the Committee issued a statement of solidarity with a letter of the Ursus workers, demanding re-instatement of their fellow employees sacked after the June events.

On 15th November, the Committee wrote to the Sejm, asking members to institute an inquiry into the following: —

1. Torture and other forms of law infringement by the police and other security services.

2. The scale of reprisals and in particular the number of persons arrested, tried by the courts and the special tribunals and of those dismissed from work.

9. Aims of the Workers Defence Committee

We repeat the statement made in Communiqué No. 3:

The Committee was formed to provide legal, financial and medical aid for the victims of reprisals. Since the trade unions, the social welfare agencies and official bodies whose duties should include the defence of workers' interests are unable or unwilling to do so, a voluntary group had to take over their responsibilities.

The Committee would consider it had no further role to play, when the appropriate institutions start performing their proper duties, when an amnesty is declared, the victimized workers are re-habilitated and re-instated in their old jobs on full pay and without loss of continuity of employment, when the scale of reprisals is made public, and when officials responsible for the abuse of law and for the use of torture are brought to court.

10. Correction

Some copies of Communiqué No. 3 included incorrectly a report that Aldona Jawłowska and Wiktor Górecki had been detained on leaving the Radom Court on 26th October. In fact, only their identity documents were examined by the police.

11. New Members of the Committee

Bogdan Borusewicz, Sopot, 23-go Marca 96 flat 24 and Józef Śreniowski, Łódź, Laurowa 2.

12. Appeal

We remind everyone again that it is a public duty to provide aid for the victims in all localities affected by the reprisals. We rely on people of courage to take immediate action and organize help wherever needed.

We appeal to the victims to use to the full the legal means of defence at their disposal.

The Committee is ready to offer help in this as far as they are able.

We appeal again for money, medical and legal aid and for reliable information. On this the work of the Committee rests.

Workers' Defence Committee: — Jerzy Andrzejewski, Stanisław Barańczak, Bogdan Borusewicz, Mirosław Chojecki, Ludwik Cohn, Jacek Kuroń, Edward Lipiński, Jan Józef Lipski, Antoni Macierewicz, Halina Mikołajska, Emil Morgiewicz, Piotr Naimski, Antoni Pajdak, Józef Rybicki, Józef Śreniowski, Aniela Steinsbergowa, Adam Szczypiorski, Wacław Zawadzki, Rev. Jan Zieja, Wojciech Ziembiński.

Supplementary information on reprisals in other localities Extracts from Communiqué No. 5

Płock: On 25th June almost the whole work force of the refinery and the petrochemical works went on strike. Every department elected representatives to take part in a general meeting which started at 10 a.m. and proceeded without incident except for a few broken windows in the Party headquarters building. About 8 p.m. the police, brought from Zgierz, intervened, dispersing the demonstrators and beating up some passers-by who were leaving the local cinema at the time. Some people were arrested and, according to official figures, 7 people were detained or fined by a special tribunal for "shouting anti-state slogans", "street brawling", "insulting the police" etc. According to our reports, in one case sentences of 3 years were given to two of the accused.

On 26th June the management ordered the strikers to work an extra 4 hours. The real reprisals started at the end of June. The Committee has so far identified 14 workers dismissed for taking part in the demonstration and the strike. The workers dismissed had also to give up their flats, which are controlled by the organization. The reasons given by the management for the dismissals varied. In one case, a seriously disabled woman worker, in receipt of an invalid pension, was accused of overturning a motor vehicle. In another, a manager denounced a subordinate for urging a street demonstration. At the subsequent hearing at the Warsaw district labour tribunal the manager admitted that on the day in question he was absent from work, but was later made to denounce the worker under threats from the personnel department. Despite that admission, the panel of judges, including Barbara Czubińska, Alicja Sęk and Makowski upheld the findings of the local tribunal. All the workers dismissed have in fact appealed to the labour tribunal, but only four of them have been reinstated.

Łódź: The strikes of 25th June did not develop into street demonstrations. In some factories workers called general meetings; in others, worker-management meetings took place. Some meetings elected delegates and prepared statements which were signed by the workers. The dismissals hit Łódź during the first week of July. We are not sure of the total figures but it seems now that the early figure of 300 was an underestimate. Workers were dismissed from "Obrońcy Pokoju", "Dywilana", "Elta", "Teofilów", "Małgorzata Fornalska", "Femina", "Elestera", "Walter", "Olimpia", "Elasticana", the Hydraulic Works, "Eskimo", "Polania" and "Anilana". The Labour Code was repeatedly broken by the management in a number of ways:

1. The appropriate trade unions were not informed about dismissals.
2. Workers absent from work on June 25th were dismissed.
3. Workers sacked were not informed of the right of appeal from the management decision.
4. Denunciation and vague rumours were considered sufficient grounds for dismissals.
5. Explanations given by the workers concerned were not recorded.
6. The dismissed workers were not allowed to surrender their tools properly and were made to leave work within two hours.

7*

Even today the employment department makes life difficult for workers who have been dismissed following the June events. As a rule they are employed only in establishments which were not involved in the strikes.

Poznań: The Roller Bearings works struck for 4 hours on June 25th. On 2 July eight workers were dismissed, four of them summarily and the other four after notice. All eight took part in the strike. They are still subjected to visits by the police who continue to question members of their families and caretakers of the flats where they live, about their present employment etc.

One decision of an appeal commission states as ground for dismissal the fact that a worker "came to work at 6.30 am., stood by his machine and discussed pay with his fellow workers."

Warsaw: We have reports about reprisals in "Żelmot", PZO,* "Kasprzak" and "Świerczewski". 200 workers have been dismissed from "Świerczewski" according to three informants.

Grudziądz report on the events of 25th June and on subsequent reprisals

From Communiqué No. 7

The workers of the No. 1 Plant in the Pomorze Foundry and Paintworks struck on that day. A few days earlier, a new wage structure was introduced in the works unfavourable for those on piece-work. After the price increases had been announced on the evening of 24th June, the night shift continued normal working. The day shift started to work in the early morning but struck at 7 a.m. The night shift workers had not yet left the works, so that both shifts were present at the time. On the 25th of each month advances on pay are available and night workers who had finished work at 6 a.m. were waiting for the pay office to open at 8 a.m. In view of the price increases the strikers demanded a return to the former norms and introduction of higher rates of pay per hour, as a condition of accepting the price increases. Most of the workforce sat-in to wait for a reply from the management to their demands. The cancellation of the price increases was an-

---

* Optical Works.

nounced at 8 p.m. and the workers started to leave. At 10 p.m. the night shift started to work normally. The strike in the No. 2 Plant did not last quite so long. The management succeeded in persuading the workers to return to work before the cancellation was announced.

We gather that there were only a few stoppages in other works in Grudziądz. In the largest works in the town, Stomil, work stopped in one section for a short time but the management quickly regained control.

The authorities in Grudziądz tried to organize mass meetings soon after the June events to censure the workers who had struck. In early July, 45 workers were sacked from the Pomorze Foundry for having taken part in the strike. No damage to the plant occurred during the strike and the only reason given for the dismissals was their refusal to work on 25th June, with an occasional rider that "as the worker concerned enjoyed the respect and confidence of his fellow workers, his refusal to work influenced others to follow his example". Among those dismissed were foremen, delegates to the Works' Council and workers with a 25 years' work record in the plant. The Works' Council presided over by Kazimierz Roszkowski (a Member of the Sejm), did not oppose the sackings. Those dismissed appealed without success to the local Labour Tribunal and to the Labour Court in Toruń. The representatives of the management, deputy personnel manager M. Betliński, K. Fijałkowski and H. Nadolski insisted that their decision to dismiss the strikers should be upheld by the court. And so it was.

Some of the workers who were sacked found new employment. They are doing unskilled jobs on low wages. The strikers who had not been sacked received, on 8th July, letters from the management informing them that, for taking part in the stoppage, they were to be reprimanded and deprived of half the annual bonus. On 29th September the reprimand was formally withdrawn, except in a few cases.

The WDC spent 111,800 zlotys in Grudziądz to assist 17 people.

Radom. Number of deaths
From Communiqué No. 7

In Communiqués 1, 2 and 3 we have reported that at least four men died in Radom during the troubles. They were:

T. Ząbecki, J. Łabędzki, Rev. Roman Kotlarz and Jan Brożyna. It seems that the number of victims was probably
higher but we are unable to give a full and reliable list. It
has been officially stated that several people committed suicide
on 25th June or therebouts. There are, however, witnesses
who maintain that they saw one of the "suicides" lying in
the street near his home in a pool of blood. His death certificate gives the cause of death as "hanging". The case of T.
Ząbecki is particularly difficult to follow: a fortnight after the
June events his family were officially informed of his death on
25th June in a fatal accident involving a tractor with a trailer.
The death certificate was not, however, available until 30th
September. There are witnesses ready to state that they were
in the same cell in the Radom prison with Ząbecki. Some
other cases are equally difficult to disentangle. The only fully
documented case, now under examination, is that of Jan
Brożyna. That this is so is due entirely to the courage of the
witnesses present when he was beaten by the police and to
the persistence of his widow who, incidentally, had been
originally told by the police that her husband died by falling
out of a window either accidentally or with the intention of
committing suicide. Witnesses of other beatings are too
frightened of the police to come forward. Several people have
been traced, however, who, separately and independently, were
able to point a location where, at night, a number of bodies
had been buried in plastic sacks, a few days after the June
events. There are also some families in Radom still waiting
for the return of their relatives who left home at the end of
June never to be heard of again. The Workers' Defence Committee is in possession of their names.

The murder of Jan Brożyna

*The circumstances surrounding the death of Jan Brożyna, who is
mentioned in the last document, as uncovered by his wife are particularly horrifying. A statement by the WDC publicised the details.*

WORKERS' DEFENCE COMMITTEE   5April 1977

STATEMENT

On 25th March Wiesława Skórkiewicz, Roman Piasecki,
and Stanisław Nowakowski were arrested on the charge of

"taking part in causing the death of Jan Brożyna". They were immediately taken to the investigation prison in Warsaw in Rakowiecka Street. The arrest warrant was signed by the Regional Deputy Prosecutor for Radom, Mr. E. Tarka.

We wish to remind our readers of the case of the murder of Jan Brożyna as described in the charge of 23 October 1976 made by Mrs. Janina Brożyna, wife of the deceased. Jan Brożyna had left home on 29 June 1976, and did not return within two days. It was a period of brutal reprisals on the Radom community, following the June disturbances.

"Together with my husband's sister, Bogumiła Bieńkowska, I began to look for my husband in various police stations. We went to the City HQ, where they said they had no detainees at all, then to the Regional HQ where it was claimed that he was not held there either. We made our way to the Magistrates' Court. We were given no information there, as it was their Saturday off work. Finally we went to the hospital. The doctor in the admissions ward asked for the date and said that no such case had been admitted. A sister wanted to check the register, but the doctor told her that he could give us the information himself. As we were going out into the corridor a woman came up to us and asked if we could identify some clothing. She took us to a room with various clothes lying in it, and we recognized my husband's clothing. We pointed to the clothing, whereupon she burst into tears and said that he was dead, that the police had brought him in with a cracked head, and that she could not work here any longer and see people suffer with damaged kidneys or eyes beaten out. I went back home and the next day, on Sunday, I went with my sister-in-law, Bronisława Skalska, to the City Headquarters. There I was told that he had been found on Koszarowa Street. I then went to the Public Prosecutor to ask for the return of the body. The Prosecutor agreed, but next day withdrew his permission, saying that he could not return the body. The day after, I went there with my husband's sisters, Bogumiła Bieńkowska and Wacława Gładek. The Prosecutor said that he himself was waiting for a decision in the matter. An hour later he granted permission to hand over the body. However, we were not allowed to dress it or to assist in dressing it; that was done behind closed doors. (...) After the funeral I went to 15 Koszarowa Street, where I found a witness who had seen my husband being beaten up. This was Wiesława Skórkiewicz, resident at 15 Koszarowa Street. She said that she had got up at two in the morning to attend to a small child, when she heard a noise. She looked out of the window and saw a man outside lying asleep. A few minutes later she got up again and saw a passing car stop. A policeman got out of it, went up to the lying man, and said: "Get up!" When the man did not react, the policeman took out his truncheon and began to beat him. Then a second policeman got out of the car and they both began to beat him. Then one said to the other: "We won't manage it, we'll have to take him in the car". They took him, unconscious, under the arms, threw him in the car and went to Werner Street which has cells for drunkards.

At the beginning of the investigation Inspector Lieutenant Młynarski from the City HQ showed me and my mother photographs of my husband's buttocks and head. There were signs of kicks and truncheon blows on the buttocks. He tried to prove that the police had nothing to do with this, and when we reminded him of the statement by Witness W. Skórkiewicz he said about her: "you believe that old bitch, she's a stupid c... and I don't take her statements into account."

The next detective from the Regional HQ told us that my husband had signs of truncheon blows on his back and an injured hand. During the identification of my husband's body, the body had been covered with a sheet up to the neck, so that I could not see any sign of beating. After some time nobody wanted to mention the fact of beating any more. I went to the station for the drunk-and-disorderly where my husband had been taken from Koszarowa Street. There I was refused any information. I emphasize at this point that according to the first version of events which we were given, my husband was taken directly from that station to the Regional hospital's resuscitation ward, on the instructions of the station doctor. Later, I was told that he had stayed in the station till the end of the night and was taken to the hospital on 30 June, at about 1 a.m., and that the doctor ascertained no serious injury, except for a black eye.

In connection with the death, my brother-in-law Stanisław Ejmowski was summoned to the Regional HQ on 12 December, where he was interrogated on the second floor. In the course of the interrogation he was blackmailed, threatened with beat-

102

ing and insulted, because he could not recall all the details.
He was held at the Regional HQ for 48 hours. Thus not only
was my husband killed, but the law was also broken in an
attempt to cover up the case. The death certificate diagnosed
fracture of the skull, haemorrages and hematomae, resulting
from injuries inflicted by other parties by means of a long, blunt
instrument. Thus there is no doubt that this was done by the
two policemen who had taken my husband from Koszykowa
Street. One of them was senior in years and according to my
information was called Staniszewski."

After eight months of silence, during which Mrs. J. Broży-
nowa was harassed and blackmailed together with her family,
the police carried out arrests. The inhabitants of 15 Koszarowa
Street were arrested, including Mrs. Skórkiewicz, who puts
the blame for the murder on the policemen. The significance
of these facts is unequivocal. One cannot resist the impression
that it is an attempt to protect the real criminals and to
intimidate the witnesses in this and other cases.
(signed by all members of the Committee)

*The official version of his death states that Mr. Brożyna had at-
tempted to rape Wiesława Skórkiewicz after he had drunk vodka with
her in her apartment. She shouted for help. Two neighbours rushed in,
murdered Brożyna and threw him out through a window.*

*At the same time, the authorities are circulating another version of
his death, partly with a view to blackmailing the deceased's family. The
murderer here is said to be Stanisław Ejmowski, a relative of Mr.
Brożyna, who is said to have been aided by another relative. The
motive was to have been the hope of inheriting Mr. Brożyna's estate.*

A dangerous legal precedent: personal responsibility for collective action

*At an appeal hearing on 10th December 1976 the Supreme Court in
Warsaw reviewed the cases of five workers who had demonstrated outside
the Radom local Party headquarters (see p. 107). At the trial the Court
upheld a questionable precedent which has consistently been applied
at other trials: personal responsibility of the accused for the collective
actions done at the demonstration. The following passage is from Communiqué No. 5.*

"... The Supreme Court found the accused guilty of
charges under article 275 para. 1 and para. 2 of the Criminal
Code, alleging hooliganism, assault, being associated with the

injuring of 75 policemen and damaging public property to the value of more than 28 million zlotys."

It appears that the accused took part in a demonstration outside the provincial Party headquarters. According to some witnesses, mostly members of the police force, the accused took part in an attempt to damage the building. The sentence of the Supreme Court, however, holds them responsible for *all* the Radom incidents of 25th June, including those which took place long after the workers' demonstration was over. In the afternoon, some people went on a rampage, looting a department store and other shops. The sum of 28 million zlotys, for which the accused are alleged to be responsible, represents the total cost of the damage, including looting. In fact, the accused took no hand in looting. Yet the Supreme Court ruled that the accused, by joining the demonstration (an "unlawful assembly"), were in a position to predict that in consequence of their acts there would be a clash with the police and that looting and damage to property would result. Therefore they were responsible for what happened. Both from the legal and from the psychological point of view such an assumption is clearly rooted in fiction.

The ruling of the Supreme Court constitutes a dangerous precedent regarding the interpretation of article 275, as it introduces a concept that demonstrators can be made collectively responsible for the criminal activities of people who, though taking no part in the demonstrations, exploit the circumstances thus created.

URSUS TRIALS

Extract from Communiqué No. 6

The trial of three Ursus workers: Marek Majewski, Jerzy Malkiewicz and Adam Żurowski, twice postponed, took place in the Warsaw Provincial Court on 29th December. The accused were charged with conspiracy to damage the railway line in order to prevent trains from using the Ursus station. The charge was brought under article 220 of the Criminal Code, which covers petty sabotage and carries sentences of between 3 and 15 years. Prior to this trial, six Ursus workers were found guilty of the same offence. In their case, the Supreme Court which, in special circumstances, is empowered to reduce sentences, reduced theirs to 1 year, suspended for 3 years.

On 29th December, only the closest relatives of the defendants were allowed to be present and the public were barred from entering despite the fact that the courtroom was half empty. M. Majewski and A. Żukowski confirmed in court that they had been beaten by the police during questioning. A. Żukowski insisted on altering the statement he had made to the police, as it had been extracted from him under duress. Some witnesses, including one named Zielonka, complained of the use of force by the police to elicit statements. The defendants Majewski and Malkiewicz asserted that on 25th June not a single representative of the management, the Party organization or the trade unions came forward to discuss the situation with the strikers. Their unwillingness to talk to the workers was the direct cause of the disturbances: when the Ursus workforce came to the conclusion that they had no other means to make their dismay over the price increases known, they blockaded and subsequently damaged the railway line. A. Żukowski claimed that on a wage of 1,900 zlotys a month, with a pregnant wife and two small children, he would not be able to feed his family if the increases were introduced. That, he said, was his motive for joining the demonstration.

The court (chairman E. Dzedzyk, judges Marat and Wargin) found all the defendants guilty. Majewski and Żukowski were sentenced to 3 years each. In the case of Malkiewicz the court used its discretion and commuted the sentence to 1 year, suspended for 3 years. It is significant that the court exercised discretion only in the case of Malkiewicz. The other two have alleged, of course, that they had been subjected to police brutality. The court chose to ignore their allegations and it admitted as evidence the statements made by Żukowski under questioning and repudiated by him in court. The sentence is subject to appeal.

WDC Guidelines on Disbursements

Extract from Communiqué No. 5

The WDC distributes legal, medical and financial help in four worker communities hit by the post-June reprisals. The communities vary and the June events took a different course in each. The situation of the victimized worker families, while always difficult, varies also a great deal. Our basic criterion in the distribution of aid is the material situation of each family and the extent of their legal costs.

The legal charges were increased drastically in 1973. At present, depending on the sentence, they are as follows:

3 months sentence — 600 zlotys; up to 6 months — 1200 zlotys; up to 1 year — 1800 zlotys; up to 2 years — 3000 zlotys; up to 5 years — 4200 zlotys; over 5 years — 6000 zlotys.

If fined, a defendant has also to pay 20% of the fine as a legal charge. In a higher court, if the court upholds the original verdict, the defendant's costs double. An application to appeal costs 1,000 zlotys. In cases connected with the June events defendants as a rule are also made to pay the costs of the trial.

The counsel's minimum rates are as follows: for a case in a district court 1200 zlotys and in a provincial court 2150 zlotys; in an appeal case in a provincial court 660 zlotys and in the Supreme Court 2150 zlotys. In addition the defendants are often made to pay a sum towards social funds, up to 5000 zlotys. Fines can be high and in the Radom trials came to as much as 3000 zlotys.

Up to 15th December the Committee has contacted 688 people and actively helped 421. We have spent 1,066,160 zlotys. So far, all this money has been collected in Poland and it continues to come in. It comes from students, the intelligentsia, peasants, industrial workers, pensioners and priests. We have been informed that a collection has been also organized abroad, where it is strongly supported by the trade unions. So far, we have not used the money collected abroad. An international committee has been formed in London and it has opened an account for incoming contributions: The Appeal for Polish Workers, A/c No. 80–1829 Irving Trust Co., 36–38 Cornhill, London E.C.3.

Members of the Workers Defence Committee have received through the PKO Bank sums totalling 2,235 dollars 14 cents, 1000 Swedish crowns and 530 Norwegians crowns. J. J. Lipski has been sent a Krugerand. The eminent artist Jan Lebensztajn has sent 12 engravings, the Nobel prize winner Heinrich Böll sent 50,000 zlotys and Max Frisch 10,000 zlotys. Those sums were royalties for their works published in Poland. We have also received 23 food parcels from abroad through

PKO. The contents were distributed among families in Radom and Ursus.

THE RADOM APPEAL TRIALS

The following article was published in Information Bulletin No. 8:

"In the name of the Polish People's Republic ..."

At the turn of 1976/77 the Supreme Court in Warsaw heard four appeal cases concerning "the most active participants of the Radom riots". At the beginning of February, at the instigation of the Party First Secretary, the State Council announced a pardon for all those convicted for their participation in the June protest. Whatever one may think of this decision, it is probably worth devoting a little time to what happened at the Supreme Court — the institution whose stance is the touchstone of Polish justice. Mr. Siła-Nowicki, the barrister, said in connection with the Radom County Court trials: "Justice is, of necessity, fragmentary; in these cases, it has been crippled." This crippledom was conclusively sanctioned by the sentences of the Supreme Court.

In Radom property and buildings were devastated; policemen sustained injuries. Edward Gierek, speaking at the beginning of February to the workers of Ursus stated that the police officers who had intervened during the June events sustained grave injuries which in some cases caused permanent disability. This is a slightly exaggerated version of events. I quote from the indictment in case no. II DS/16/76/S at the County Court in Radom: "75 police officers sustained bodily injuries in the course of the riots. Of these, the following sustained *serious* injuries: Antoni Adamowicz — first and second degree burns on the right thigh and burns on both hands; Dariusz Krajewski — concussion of the brain; Henryk Falkowski — bruising of the lower and upper lip; Witold Żmudziński — injury of the collar-bone; Henryk Tomczyk — bruising of the left temple with haematoma; Jan Mózg — injury of the right knee-joint; Witold Różanek — injury of the left eyeball and injury of eyelids with haematoma; Kazimierz Nowak — haematoma of the right knee-joint." *That is all* that is to be found concerning the injuries in the indictment: bruises, surface injuries, no fractures, no internal damage.

107

The same text with the same names is repeated verbatim in all four indictments. I have taken the liberty of quoting this over-long and boring item, since otherwise no one would have been prepared to believe that the other police officers, named in the full case records, complained of: neurosis, stomach pains, abrasion and bruising of the right wrist. Nonetheless there *were* injuries and someone had to be punished. The aim of "punishing someone", of "giving a deterrent example" was the key to the entire investigative and judicial procedure, from the Magistrates and Regional Courts to the Supreme Court. This was to be the purpose served by the "łapanka" — there is no reason to shy from this word* — organised by the police, as the result of which 2,000 people were detained in Radom in the last days of June. Then there were Magistrates' Courts, and Courts of Summary Justice, handing out sentences left right and centre. How did this take place? One person who took part has given an account of how he was allocated to a group which was to be summarily tried by a court. Another group was to go up before the Magistrate; one of its members, however, could not put his trousers on because his legs were so swollen from a beating. Time pressed, however, so the groups were switched round. That is not mere crippledom of justice — it is callous vengeance. Can one, in such circumstances, talk of correct preparatory procedure? When "health trots" are in operation in the police and prison cells? One of the detainees relates: "... it was dark ... At first, we couldn't tell what they'd thrown into the cell ... a blanket? A mattress? It turned out it was Gniadek ... he looked nothing like a human being at all ... He wanted to hang himself ... said he couldn't stand it any longer ..." The same accounts were told by everyone who had been detained, everyone who was convicted. Everyone in Radom knows about it, but the Supreme Court does not. It knows nothing and can know nothing about the charges and complaints which have been sent in by the people of Radom and have filled the spacious litter-bins of the Public Prosecution Department; but it cannot have not noticed the contradictions with which the case records are teeming and which provide evidence of the chaos and hysteria which befell the investigative authorities

---

* The Polish word "łapanka" immediately conjures up the arbitrary round-ups made during the War by the Nazis. (Translator's note.)

after the June events. It is not surprising that over 2000 people were detained. It is even difficult to say of the Radom · trials that they were rigged, since so little effort was made to maintain even a semblance of legality. The chaos of the preparative phase, whose motto was "punishment as an example · to all", was allowed to flow along all the judiciary channels, from court to court, without encountering a single obstacle. Police witnesses could be in different places at the same time (vide Ōpolski and Majak), or could ascribe the same action to different people in different cases, and their testimonies were always relied on so long as they condemned the person in question. Not even documents stating that the defendants could not have committed a given offence because by that time they had already been detained (Zabrowski, Gutowski) could shake the policemen's testimony. "What reason could they possibly have for making false statements, after all?" — asked the Court. It is, indeed, hard to think of one, but my guess would be that the reason was simply to supply a quota of defendants for exemplary punishment. In an atmos-- phere of complete contempt for the law and total indolence in conducting the preliminary investigation, the Radom police had neither the possibilty nor the desire to find the real culprits, and quickly gave the courts the required quota.

The sole aim of the police was to compromise and discredit the workers' demonstration, and that was best achieved with the help of hardened recidivists. Again, the likelihood of the indictment was immaterial. At the time of the disturbances Mr. Grudzień had a broken hand and ribs, so his activity must necessarily have been limited; his criminal record, however, played the decisive role and he adorned the dock in the first trial. By the time of the fourth trial, the police had run out of hardened criminals. So, after three weeks Chomicki was arrested. Lieutenant Dalbiak, who had known him earlier, saw him wrecking the Party HQ, but it took him all of three weeks to remember it, despite having met him in the street in the meantime. Afterwards, however, his memory was perfect. Then there is the absurdity of the charge made against Gniadek — that he had set fire to the Party building with the aid of some newspapers. Should anyone have his doubts, please conduct the following experiment: take a large number of weeklies and books — as Gniadek is charged with doing in his indictment — and try to set fire to them without using petrol or meths.

It is a task which takes several hours. The court, however, could not perceive the absurdity of the accusation. One can understand many things but it is impossible to understand how all this could have escaped the attention of the Supreme Court and how verdicts of guilty could have been pronounced on the basis of such evidence.

Nevertheless in the present situation it is not perhaps even the immediate injustice committed against the defendants that is the most important aspect; it will, at any rate, be partly alleviated by the State Council's pardon. I do not deny that some of the accused were indeed present at the scene of the riots, and that perhaps the actions committed by one or two of the accused may by a coincidence — I emphasize, by a pure coincidence — correspond to the actions imputed to them in the indictment. These may indeed repent (the pardon, as the Party First Secretary said in Ursus, would apply only to those who showed their "repentance"). But how are those who were convicted unjustly to show their repenttance? How can they do this without debasing their dignity and without covering up the lawlessness which occurred after the Radom events? Let us hope that in this case, too, the leadership will display a liberal attitude and compensate the people for the wrongs committed against them.

There remains, then, one more issue, which cannot be made good by any act of pardon — the issue of the precedent set by the verdicts of the Supreme Court. In these, the Supreme Court departed from the principle of the individualization of offences and legalized the application of collective responsibility. According to the principle applied by the Supreme Court anyone who does not leave a mass gathering should anticipate all its consequences and answer before the law for all the losses caused in its wake.

Still another issue is the combination in the Radom cases of Article 275 of the Penal Code (rowdy gathering) with Article 59 (acts of vandalism) which causes the lower limit of imprisonment to be raised $1\frac{1}{2}$ times and does not permit a reduction of the sentence, except in particular cases. A verdict of guilty pronounced on the basis of Article 59 requires the defendant to have acted without reason, or for trivial reason. So it appears that the Radom events occurred without reason. Ten thousand people demonstrated without reason? Absurd. Let us suppose, then — as the Supreme Court did — that

110

they did have a reason. "But those who wrecked the Party HQ, what reason could they have? If they had wanted an improvement in the material situation, they would not have destroyed property..." — thus the Supreme Court Judge Polony justified his verdict. The cries of "Red Bourgeoisie" raised by the demonstrators outside the Party buildings are perhaps the best reply to this. The ham and meat which were taken outside from the Party HQ buffet and which make frequent reappearances in the records of the various cases were the very reason why a workers' demonstration was turned into a riot at which acts of theft were committed. Social injustice has been the cause of a number of revolutions in the past and I would think it difficult to consider it a trivial reason, in compliance with Article 59 of the Penal Code. (The indictments reveal, incidentally, that the buffet in the Party Regional HQ also served beer, in violation of an instruction made by the Council of Ministers. To think of the number of tears shed by Załuski and other top dignitaries over their colleagues going off for "a beer or two" during working hours!)

And finally a third issue — the combination of the previous two articles with Article 60 of the Penal Code (reversion to crime). The article in question states unequivocally that reversion to crime occurs when the defendant commits an offence of a similar nature to his previous offence. So the court displays its full talent at acrobatics to prove that, e.g., petty theft is an offence similar in character to participating in a rowdy gathering as defined in Article 275. The fact that Article 275 occurs in Chapter XXXVI of the Penal Code — which concerns itself with offences against the public order and contains, in general, articles of a political nature *par excellence* — is immaterial. What is material is to make the sentenced suffer, to terrorise the public.

The defendants are referred to as the dregs of society. It is unfortunately not the case that being up before the law is as rare a phenomenon as the Supreme Court would have it be. Statistical records show that 14% of men under 21 years of age have been sentenced by juvenile courts or public courts. I do not know the figures for older persons. It is also common knowledge that delinquency is greater in town communities than it is in the country. It is difficult to call such a section of the community its "dregs". Later such people come to lead a more stable life, set up families and, provided, no obstacle is placed in their path, return to society. They are certainly not helped in this by such sentences as have been passed in the Radom cases. Z.Z.

THE SECOND WAVE OF WORKERS' PROTESTS

· *The workers in Poland possess no platform on which to challenge the injustices of the courts and the brutality of the police. In the face of the reprisals which followed the disturbances of 1970 on the Coast, they could but remain helpless and mute. In the aftermath of June 1976, however, a new phenomenon emerged: there came a second wave of protest. Workers took up their pens and wrote appeals and complaints to the highest authorities. Without doubt such a course of action would have appeared hopeless, if the workers had not been conscious that they were not alone in their plight and that people elsewhere in the country were not indifferent to their fate. This second protest was almost immediately to be reinforced by a campaign of petitions, instigated by the WDC, appealing to Parliament that a Commission of Inquiry be established in order to examine the behaviour of the courts and of the police. The militia attempted by the use of bribes, threats and harassment to force workers to withdraw their complaints. In some cases they may have succeeded, but often the complaints were re-affirmed. Stanisław Wijata mentioned on p. 128 is a case in point.*

Chomicki's case is of particular interest. He was arrested three weeks after the Radom demonstration and, presumably because of an earlier conviction, was made into a scapegoat for the acts of vandalism which were arranged by the authorities or genuinely accompanied the demonstration (cf. page 61). He was sentenced to 9 years' imprisonment on extremely doubtful evidence. In a bid to secure justice, he has been staging a number of hunger-strikes in prison and though over 6ft tall now weighs only 8 stone.

Majewski (cf. WDC Communiqué No. 6) was one of those to be accused of derailing a traction engine in Ursus. As a result of police beatings, he sustained two jaw fractures and lay incapacitated in a police hospital for four months.

Letter of the 889 workers of Ursus

To the Government of
the Polish People's Republic   4 November 1976

We, the workers of the URSUS Motor works appeal [to the Government of the People's Republic of Poland] that all those who were dismissed from work as a result of the strike and demonstrations of 25th June 1976, be reinstated.

We consider this indispensable in view of the country's economic predicament, the tense atmosphere at our Works, and, our present production difficulties caused by shortage of experienced personnel.

We appeal that they be reinstated on the same conditions of employment as previously and with full enjoyment of all privileges connected with continuity of employment and that their pay be backdated to cover their period of unemployment.

We are convinced that only then will we be in a position, in common effort with our countrymen, to face the difficult economic situation in which our country finds itself.

See the WDC's "Appeal to the Nation" for the repercussions of this letter (p. 127).

Letter of the 67 tortured workers of Radom

To the Chief Public Prosecutor,
Lucjan Czubiński. Warsaw, 1st December 1976
Al. 1-ej Armii Wojska Polskiego 16/24.

Dear Sir,

I enclose a copy of a letter of complaint from the Radom workers, who have deposited the original with me. I vouch for the authenticity of the text and the signatures.

Yours faithfully,
Władysław Bieńkowski

To the Chief Public Prosecutor,
Lucjan Czubiński. Radom, 30th November 1976

In reply to the "Statement from the Chief Public Prosecutor" in *Życie Warszawy* we, the undersigned, declare that the Chief Public Prosecutor has been grossly misinformed and that it is not true that "all the cases have been considered with great care, both as regards the offence and the person of the offender, during investigation by the police and the Examining Magistrates before the hearing and in the course of the trial itself."

We declare that, when arrested after the incidents of 25th June, we were beaten by the police. Each of us had to run at least once through the so called "health trots", i.e. a cordon of uniformed and plain-clothed police, who beat and kicked us. Every time we were transferred to another place we were beaten while getting in and out of the police trucks. During the interrogation we were tortured, so that we would make the statement they wanted. In the Radom prison and when detained in the Radom police headquarters, we were beaten by the police and the prison warders.

We demand that those responsible should be punished. We also submit that there is a clear case for a Sejm Commission to inquire into the way in which basic principles of the rule of law have been violated.

67 signatures follow

Complaint from Czesław Chomicki

Młodzianowskiego 16/33

Radom.

To the Chief Public Prosecutor's Office, Polish People's Republic.

REQUEST

I appeal to you to look with the greatest possible care into my case, as I had a very grave injury done to me when I was charged in connection with the events of 25th June 1976.

On 13th August I appeared before the Provincial Court, Criminal Division. I was sentenced to 9 years' imprisonment and to pay costs for an offence under article 275 §1 and §2 of the Criminal Code. I was charged with maliciously damaging the building occupied by the Radom Party headquarters. In effect, I was really sentenced for all the offences committed in Radom on that day: the assault on the police, arson, theft, damage to public property and all.

This is how it happened. On 21st April 1976 I was released from prison in Kalisz where I had served a 3 year sentence. I joined my wife and four-year-old son in Radom in a flat at Młodzianowska 16, Flat 33. My main aim was to break completely with criminal circles. I found a job as a lathe operator in the Radom Vehicle Repairs Works. My wife worked between 10 a.m. and 6 p.m. and our day was planned as follows: I went to work at 6 a.m. and my wife at 10 a.m., having taken the boy to his nursery school. I then collected him on my way from work and we returned home together. At home, I took care of the child and of various domestic chores. I took the boy for walks, did some furniture repairs and so on. At 5.45 p.m. I went to collect my wife from the shop where she worked and we returned together to our home where our son, left in the care of my father-in-law, was awaiting us. We prepared our supper together and after supper we either watched the television or went for an evening walk. I soon became known at work as a conscientious, willing and

114

disciplined worker. I wished to learn as much as possible and to make up for all the time I had wasted. I wished to become a useful member of society, and to regain people's confidence. I was going to start a course at the Technical College in September and the management in the Works promised to help me in this plan. I quickly came to believe again in people and in human kindness and helpfulness. I had hopes that this faith would stay with me for life. I was well aware how much I had missed by being sent to prison three times for a total of seven and a half years. My wife opened my eyes to a different, good and honest world and I owe everything to her steadfastness. Every false step of mine was put straight by her.

This happy life lasted until 25th June. On that day I lost everything. It was a very strange day. I started work as usual, at 6 a.m. At the Works, I found great excitement concerning the increase in food prices. I clocked in and I went to my bench. I worked until 10 a.m., although some workers stopped earlier. When the incidents started, I went to the foreman Marian Czyż and asked for a pass out to be able to see my doctor. I thought that was the best thing to do in my case: as an old lag I had to keep out of any possible trouble. The foreman signed my pass and I left the Works for the shop where my wife worked. I told her what happened. The manageress of the shop was present at our conversation. My wife agreed that I had done right and I went home. Soon afterwards my wife also returned, as they had decided to close the shop because of the trouble in the streets. We thought that we would go to visit our relations living at Sowińska 7 and Filtrowa 15. We left the flat about 2.50 p.m.

We saw a large crowd in May Day Street near the Forestry Department (I did not know that the Party had moved into that building). The street was blocked by vehicles and we had to make our way through the crowd. Someone shouted that there were people inside. At that moment I saw smoke escaping from the building. I told my wife to stay where she was while I went inside. I still thought that the building belonged to the Forestry Department and I knew that the people inside needed help. I cannot describe what I saw inside. The interior was a shambles and the ground floor was on the point of catching fire. Only then I realised that it must have been the result of the rioting and I was about to go back when I saw a man trying to stop the crowd from doing further damage. I decided to help him: I started getting people away, sometimes even using force with those who would not listen. I wanted to make it clear that my intentions were good and to justify my being in the building at all by saving as much public property as I could, particularly as I recognized among the crowd some plain-clothes police. I wanted to make clear that I had nothing to do with people intent on destroying the place although I found myself among them. I was very conscious that because of my record I could easily be suspected of trouble-making. The man who first made the effort to stop further destruction is called Tadeusz Żabicki and lives at Struga 4. Together, we got hold of fire extinguishers and tried to make them work but we found that they were not in proper working order. Throughout all this, we were under observation by Mieczysław Pierzchała from the police, who later said in court that he did not remember me, although he remembered Żabicki as the person who tried to put out the fire and save the building. Żabicki and I managed to get up to the first floor to fetch more extinguishers which were lying along the wall. When we were about to take them up, a man in the centre of a group of people told us to leave them alone as they were out of order and to leave the building. I knew the man: he was a policeman called Dalbiak. I had dealings with him in 1972 and he told me then that if I ever got out of prison he would put me inside again. He kept his word: during my trial he gave evidence, false evidence, that I took part in wrecking the building.

I wanted so much to show my good intentions and to avoid bringing suspicion upon myself, but I became a scapegoat for the whole crowd just the same. My past wrecked the good I tried to do. Will I ever be able to become a member of society, however hard I try?

The smoke increased and Żabicki and I decided to leave the building. We left through the back entrance. Just then someone in the crowd outside shouted that there were some people still left on the top floor and that they should be warned. I rushed back into the building, followed by Żabicki. The smoke was getting thick. Żabicki found it hard to breathe, he had to slow down and finally to stop. I managed to get to the top floor where I raised the alarm shouting that everyone should leave by the back way, as the front was on fire. The smoke forced me to run down. Żabicki joined me on the way and we left the building together. I was very tired and choking through the smoke when I joined my wife who was waiting outside. We decided to go home instead of visiting our relatives.

Altogether, I must have spent 15 minutes inside the building. I told my wife what I saw and did while there, how I tried to save things. I also told her about my fears that I might be suspected of trouble-making because I was seen inside and some people might not realize that she was there with me, although waiting in the street. My wife thought that I was oversensitive on that point.

The following days were peaceful. I went to work and looked after the boy and our home as usual until 10th August.

On that day, my father came in as we were planning to go fishing together. I left the boy with my father and went to see a neighbour who was going to join us on the fishing trip. On my return my sister told me that a man was there to see me; a car was parked outside and I knew that it was the police. I had nothing on my conscience so I walked straight in. I was arrested and taken to the Provincial Police Headquarters and questioned as to how I spent 25th June. I told them all about that day including what happened inside the Party building.

I was charged with taking part in wrecking of the building. The man Dalbiak whom I saw in the building on 25th June, caught me by the hair and banged my head on the desk. I was then beaten and knocked about and told that, innocent or not, I was going to be put inside, as people like me were not to be trusted and Radom had to be cleaned up. They told me that I should be glad I was to be charged only with wrecking; if I talked too much they would add arson and theft. I knew then that I had no chance, but to this day I do not understand why I was treated in this way. I live in a socialist country and I know what socialism stands for. I have been treated unjustly but I know that someone will look into this. The Party leads the Nation and represents us and I appeal for justice to the Party organization.

I desire to be a decent person and not an enemy of my country, I have left a wife and a four-year-old son outside.

I know that I have been tried for crimes I have not committed. I don't think this is right. I may have a bad record, but I am a human being, a man like the rest and I want to live like the rest. I have done wrong in the past and I have been punished for it. Why should I now be punished again for trying to live a decent life? I will appeal to every institution in Poland and abroad, I will keep at it for as long as I am able. If I fail I shall die cursing those who did it to me. I am appealing to all the legal organizations in the world, to the International Organization for Human Rights and all the others.

I do not blame anybody except the police who gave false evidence against me. They said I took part in the wrecking and yet they could not say how I was dressed that day. One said I wore grey trousers and a dark shirt and another remembered me in blue trousers and a light coloured shirt. Tadeusz Żabicki was not in court, although he was the only person with me at the critical time. The police said at first that Żabicki tried to save the building but as soon as they heard that I wanted Żabicki to be called they changed their evidence: they made a statement to the effect that Żabicki took a hand in the wrecking and even that he was detained for it on 26th June. In fact Żabicki had sent in a statement saying that we tried together to stop the damage. According to the police that document had got lost. Anyhow, the police had warned Żabicki that if he appeared in court as my witness he would also be arrested and although I tried to have him called on three occasions, he did not appear.

A policeman whom I called as my witness did not appear until the third hearing. He spoke well of Żabicki but as to me, he said that I had been one of the wreckers and that he did not see any action on my part to save the building. That policeman did not wish to harm me but was afraid of losing his job.

My wife managed to find Żabicki and together with my father tried to persuade him to give evidence on my behalf. He told them that the police had threatened to implicate him in a murder committed on 8th June in Waryński Street if he did so.

I appeal to you for a retrial. For 15 days after the disturbances I stayed at home and yet I was not arrested until 8th August, although the charge was serious enough to rate a nine year sentence. Why was I not arrested straight away for that serious crime? Is it because time was needed to prepare false evidence? One policeman, later a witness for the prosecution, met me twice in the street during that period. I was alone on one occasion and with my wife on another. The name of the policeman is Dalbiak. Why did he not arrest me then and there if he saw me committing the offence?

I appeal to all the legal organizations in Poland and abroad and to the International Organization for Human Rights to intervene on my behalf.

Czesław Chomicki

Complaint by Ireneusz Majewski

Bohaterów Warszawy 42/41,
05810 Ursus
2nd January 1977

To the Sejm Commission for Home Affairs and Justice

The time has come for my voice to join all the others to appeal to the above mentioned Commission. We ask it to name a Special Commission of the Sejm to examine and let the public know about the June events. Also, to punish the guilty representatives of the authorities who tortured both the strikers and those not on strike in Ursus and outside Ursus.

STATEMENT

On 25th June last year I witnessed what happened on the railway tracks in Ursus between 11 a.m. and 8.30 p.m. It was a very hot day, bad for my health as I have had two coronaries: the first in May and another on 20th June. I tried to stay in the shade and I saw what happened from a nearby wood. In the beginning I did not notice any police around the place. If they were there, they could have stopped what happened later. Up till 2 p.m. the workers sat on the railway line. I have been told that they were waiting for someone from the Government to come and discuss with them the reasons for the food prices going up. As I have said, nothing happened until 2 p.m., except that the trains were stopped. By 2 o'clock, the workers understood that nobody was going to come (a helicopter was flying overhead but they couldn't get in touch with the pilot). At the time some of the workers started to rip up railway lines. They had no tools to start with but they wanted to keep the lines blocked. I think that they had it in mind that it was the only way to get somebody from the Government to come and talk to them. But not even derailing

119

one engine and then another brought anybody in authority to them. The police did not come, either, to try and stop the damage. It was well after 8 p.m. and a large group of workers were still standing about (my brother and I were on the outside of the group), when we were surprised by some civilians who swooped down on us with clubs, hitting out right, left and centre. I got one on the back of my head so that it started spinning and my brother Marek who had turned round to see what was happening to me caught it on the face. Only when I got him home unconscious we discovered that all his teeth were loose. I then took him to the first aid place in Warsaw. The First Aid sent us to a hospital in Lindley Street. They found there that his jaw was cracked in two places. They had to operate to take out some teeth and to wire him up; it took them 4 hours. They started at 11 o'clock and didn't finish till 3 o'clock in the morning.

We returned home in the morning and our parents told us that six policemen had searched the flat and we could see the mess they had left behind. I can't think what they were looking for. I then took my brother to a summer chalet I was renting in Michałowice near Ursus. I spent the time cooking him soups and other liquids because he had to be fed through a rubber tube. I took him every day to have penicillin injections ordered by the doctor. On 1st July, five days after the disturbances, we were resting at the chalet, both wearing only shorts because of the heat. Suddenly we saw the police arriving with revolvers at the ready. Six of them entered the chalet and the rest surrounded it. They ordered us to dress. We dressed, were handcuffed, marched into two cars, with a third car in front and another behind. We were taken to the police headquarters in Ursus. The handcuffs were taken off and we were ordered in. The police, armed with clubs, were lined up on each side of the stairs leading into the building. I was going in first and it was easy to guess what was going to happen. As I reached the third step, I had already as much as I could take, so I ran in and for a moment I fell unconscious. As I lay on the floor I was kicked, then they took my clothes and left me in only briefs and a white shirt. Then I was thrown into a cell. I felt pain under the breast bone coshed and knocked about? They knew very well that I was and I knew another coronary was on the way. Why was I an invalid after two coronaries. I would like the honourable Commission to explain this to me.

My brother followed me up the stairs and got the same treatment although they could not help seeing that his face was wired up. He could not even ask them to stop as he was not able to speak and he had to watch what was being done to me. After I was thrown into a cell, he saw my shoes lying in the entrance hall. Those shoes have still not been returned to me.

As I am putting all this down, I remember that I got the same treatment from the Gestapo during the war. That time we were also beaten up without any explanation and we saw bodies being dragged away.

The police took away the medicines I always have to carry with me and no one took any notice of my groans. When I came to, I saw a woman in white leaning over me. This was the casualty doctor whom someone called. She got my nitroglycerine back from the police and gave it to me but it did not work and I heard her tell them that she would have to take me to a hospital straight away. They pulled on my trousers, got hold of my arms and legs and carried me to a police van outside. They threw me in like an animal for slaughter and I was rushed to the police headquarters in Warsaw with the horn going full blast. I was put on a stretcher there and carried into a surgery. They took a cardiograph and decided to take me to a hospital. This time we drove in a proper ambulance and I lay on the bed in it. The lady doctor was again with me; I did not see her in the Black Maria. I only remember Sergeant Gołąbczyk was there trying to lift my eyelids to see if I was still alive.

I was taken to the Mokotów prison hospital with my third coronary. 23 days later, when they had brought me back to life, I was transferred from the hospital to an ordinary prison. My brother and I had already been tried under lynch law on 25th June and again on 1st July. Why was it necessary after all that for my brother to be brought before the Provincial Court on 29th December after 4 months in a prison hospital and yet another jaw operation made necessary by the beating up at the police station? Hadn't they punished him enough just for standing by during the strike on 25th June? His prison hospital card shows that he was brought in covered in bruises from a heavy beating. The court gave him 3 years. How can any man in our country be punished three times in this way for the same offence?

In prison I asked as soon as I could for a medical inspection of the bruises on my back and shoulders and of the black and blue marks I had all the way from the small of my back down to my right knee. Nothing was done and on the fourth day, when I was being questioned by Captain Buczkowski of the Warsaw Police Headquarters I showed him my bruises. He only remarked: "they should not beat people up". Where was he when other policemen did it? And why didn't he do something about it?

On the fifth day I was questioned by Prosecutor Barcewska. I showed her my bruises again but she didn't bat an eyelid. Obviously, she though that it was right and proper for the police to apply lynch law to people, whether guilty of anything or not. She was not going to do anything at all to stop it happening again and again as a part of the administration of justice.

Those people who ruined my health and nearly cost me my life were product of the *People's Republic!* The people put them where they are, but they have turned against their own. There were men like 2nd Lieutenant Janusz Duszczyk (District Police Headquarters Praga-Południe, at Grenadierów 73/77), or like Sergeant Gołąbczyk and Kujawa, Woźniak, Warsiński, Mieczysław Przybyłek, themselves all from Ursus. These men were allowed to beat up helpless men already suffering from other injuries. They were given power to cosh and kick men who were hardly able to stand up. Their victims spent their lives working to pay for the keep and the weapons for such as them. The weapons they now used on their backs. It has happened to me, to my brother Marek and to many, many others.

In the end Dr. Okoński made an official inspection of my injuries at the prison hospital. I have also six other witnesses in Medical Ward No. 4 of that hospital, who can confirm what I looked like when they brought me in.

Perhaps the members of the police would like me to greet them with a smile when I pass them in the street? No such luck. Never, I say. And so do all the other who had the same treatment. There were many of us. I write on behalf of my brother, now in prison, and on behalf of them all. My brother has been allowed out for a day to bury our mother on 9th December and he is likely to be out again to bury our father who is 74 years old and has no one to look after him as I myself am in need of care. For the last ten years I have been suffering from diabetes, a bad back and recently I have had three coronaries.

I say it again: on behalf of all the victims of the police I demand the setting up of a Special Sejm Commission to deal with the guilty.

I remain hopeful of a positive reply as my hold on life is not very strong and I may not last long enough to get one. I have, so far, waited in vain for a reply from the Chief Public Prosecutor's Office and from the Chairman of the Council of State.

I am informing the Workers' Defence Committee of the contents of this letter.

Ireneusz Majewski

THE CAMPAIGN FOR A PARLIAMENTARY COMMISSION OF INQUIRY

On 15th November 1976 the Workers' Defence Committee petitioned Parliament to establish a Commission of Inquiry into the behaviour of police and security organs and the judiciary over the June events, The WDC simultaneously appealed to the nation to support this initiative. The response so far totals 3000 signatures: individual letters (for example from Bieńkowski) and in collective petitions such as by 28 eminent professors, members of the Polish Academy of Sciences (late additions brought the figure to 34), 172 intellectuals, writers, actors (increased later to 296), 185 priests from the diocese of Przemyśl. Student petitioners numbered over 1,600 (231 from Gdańsk, 730 from Warsaw, 285 from the Catholic University of Lublin, 517 from Cracow). The figure of 3000 is not large in comparison with the estimated 40,000 in the constitutional issue; what is perhaps significant is the calibre of some of the signatories.

The nearest to an official response was a statement made on 5th January 1977 by the Procurator General before a Parliamentary Commission for Internal Affairs. He claimed that the complaints were falsifications and the allegations of beatings were unfounded.

THE WORKERS' DEFENCE COMMITTEE

Warsaw, 15th November 1976
To the Sejm of the Polish People's Republic

Appeal

' The Workers' Defence Committee appeals to the Sejm to initiate proceedings leading to the establishment of a Commission of Inquiry into the strikes and mass demonstrations of June 1976 and in particular into:

1. Torture and other forms of infringement of the law by the police and the security services.

2. The scale and extent of reprisals, the total figures of those arrested, imprisoned, sentenced by the courts and by special tribunals and dismissed from work.

The facts

The Workers' Defence Committee examined 96 cases of detention in Radom and 94 in Ursus. 93 of those detained in Radom and 46 in Ursus claimed that they were beaten up and their families testified that they had seen marks left by the beatings. Only 4 people reported that they had not been maltreated.

All reports follow a similar pattern. The detainees in Radom were taken to District or Local Police Headquarters and in Ursus to the local police station, where they were made to march or run the gauntlet, the so-called "health-trot" i.e. through a double row of uniformed and plain-clothes policemen brandishing truncheons. "Health trots" were organized repeatedly throughout the period of arrest and imprisonment. The reports agree that during pre-trial examination the suspects were beaten, hit and kicked to extract confessions. Some of the arrested suffered severe injuries and had to be removed to hospital.

Some detainees were moved in refrigerated trucks designed for the transport of food. People lost consciousness through lack of air. Most victims lack courage to bring formal complaints. However, we have been told that the following lodged complaints with the Chief Prosecutors' Office and with the Sejm Commission for Home Affairs: Czesław Chomicki, Zbigniew Cibor, Waldemar Gutowski, Jan Milczar, Janina Nazimek on behalf of her son, Ryszard Nowak, Jan Szczepański. In a submission sent to the Sejm Commission for Home Affairs and Justice, Janina Brożyna described in great detail the circumstances of her husband's death following a beating by the police. The authorities' routine answer to the complaints is that, following detailed inquiries, it has been found that the police intervention was fully justified and its conduct was within the law. The case of Mirosław Chmielewski is an exception. While under examination in a District Court in Warsaw, Chmielewski declared (on 16th July) that he had been subjected to protracted torture by the police. On 27th September, at the trial in the Supreme Court of Chmielewski and others, the defence submitted medical evidence to that effect and the Public Prosecutor promised an inquiry into their allegations.

The facts, then, are well-known and yet no steps have been taken by the authorities to bring the guilty to justice. On the contrary, the Chief Public Prosecutor found it appropriate to praise the police before a Sejm Commission. In Radom, of all places, an anniversary of the Police and the Security Service was celebrated with a march and, according to the press, a gift of a new banner was made to them by the local population.

The brutality of the police does not indicate that they have been taught to respect either the rule of law or the rights of an individual. The frequency with which "health trots" have been used in Radom and Ursus leads one to suspect that this is a part of police training. In general the cases quoted demonstrate improper and, indeed, intolerable behaviour by the police. It will be necessary, therefore, for the Commission to direct its attention to an investigation not only of the behaviour of individual policemen, but also of the methods of training and the in-service regulations now in force.

The majority of the Radom and Ursus cases were tried by Special Tribunals. In the early cases sentences consisted mostly of a fine and of dismissal from work. However, the police frequently appealed against the light sentences; retrials were ordered and followed in most cases by a sentence of two or three months and often by a fine as well. In a number of cases defendants were sentenced several times for the same offence. The Special Tribunal hearings were usually restricted to a reading of a police statement recommending a verdict of guilty followed by the passing of sentence.

125

In Radom, where greater numbers were involved, even verdict of guilty followed by the passing of sentence.
that procedure was abandoned for a simpler one: the accused were given a document to sign, containing the sentence, and the trial was over. Some of those sentences were later repealed on the grounds of a manifest infringement of the law by the Minister of Justice and some cases were re-tried. Clearly all the cases heard by Special Tribunals should be looked into by the Commission.

Not only Tribunals, but also the Courts were guilty of irregularities. It became a rule in Radom for the Courts to rely exclusively on the evidence of the police and the security service. On many occasions the police were unable to give the Courts sufficient grounds for identifying a defendant. They would say that he or she was among the crowd of demonstrators shouting abuse and throwing stones and an assertion of this kind would pass for evidence. Many suspects were not arrested at the time of the "crime", but hours or even days later.

In many cases complaints made in Court about the use of physical violence by the police were ignored by the judges. The most common charge in Radom was hooliganism: "the accused joined a crowd with the intent to assault the police, damage public buildings and private property. As a result, 75 policemen suffered injury and the damage was estimated at 28 million zlotys". This kind of charge meant that an element of collective responsibility was introduced and the people were tried not for what they had done themselves but for all that had happened in Radom on 25th June. We are now in a position to quote cases tried in the District Court there, when the same defendant had to answer the same charge twice and was sentenced twice for it. The Court ignored objections raised by the defence, although the repetition of charges was clearly outside the law.

The exact scale of reprisals is still unknown. We have no doubt that the victims we have been able to contact represent only a fragment of the total figure. The public have reason to think that the numbers involved are much greater than they have been led to believe so far. The social risks of a situation where the police break the law which it is their duty to uphold, are very great indeed.

126

The number of dismissals from work appears also to be greater than originally thought and to have occurred all over the country. The authorities interpret article 52 of the Labour Code as an anti-strike measure, clearly an infringement on their part of article 68 of the Constitution.

The country fears the return of Stalinist brutality and oppression. The exposure of abuses, punishment of those responsible and a compensation for the victims are the essential preconditions for return to the rule of law.

The above considerations lead the Committee to present this document to the Sejm and to the public.

The Workers' Defence Committee

The Appeal, accompanied by a letter, was sent to the President of the Sejm by A. Pajdak on 16th November 1976.

THE WORKERS' DEFENCE COMMITTEE
Appeal to the Nation

Five months have passed since the brutal suppression of the workers' demonstrations and strikes, followed by numerous trials and mass dismissals from work. The Workers' Defence Committee was set up in response to that situation. Social solidarity made the provision of financial, legal and medical assistance possible. It helped those persecuted to endure a most critical time. 230 families are receiving continuous assistance. 658 thousand zlotys had been paid out before 22nd November. Hundreds receive legal aid from lawyers who offer to provide it as a social duty. Hundreds of people are giving their time and skills to assist the victims of reprisals. Medical help is offered, funds are being raised, information is collected, trials are attended, the Committee's communiqués copied and handed out. On 4th November 1976, 889 workers of the Ursus Mechanical Works sent a letter to the highest authorities of the Polish State, demanding re-instatement of all those dismissed from work for their part in the June protests. Evidence of wide social support encouraged this move. Workers are venturing to claim their rights, and to appeal to the courts against management decisions, those imprisoned appeal against sentences passed during the initial wave of reprisals. Some of those beaten up and tortured have issued complaints demanding that the truth be told and justice

127

be done. It might have been expected that the authorities would respond in genuine social interest to these requests and complaints and reveal in a public statement the whole truth about the June events. Instead, a new campaign of repression, terror and intimidation is being waged. At the Ursus works representatives of management and members of the Party machine, and in some cases police agents, are conducting numerous interrogations of workers who have signed the letter to the authorities demanding reinstatement of their sacked comrades. The workers interrogated are being pressed to reveal the names of colleagues who drafted the letter and collected the signatures. Threats are used to induce signatories to withdraw their names. In Radom police and security agents visit homes of the victims and put pressure on them to refrain from official complaints. Those who have already dared to issue such complaints have been subjected to interrogations lasting for several hours. They are asked to give the names of the people who came to talk to them, the amount of financial assistance accepted, and to withdraw the complaint under threat of further reprisals. At least six people have been subjected to such interrogations, including Janina Brożyna, whose husband, Jan Brożyna, was murdered during the night of 29 to 30 June 1976. She has sent a complaint about the interrogation to the Parliamentary Committee for Home Affairs and Justice and to the Public Prosecutors' Office. People who are being threatened now, had to endure torture in June and may be sensitive to intimidation. Fortified by widespread social support and solidarity, they ventured to tell the truth about what they experienced. Now they have come under pressures designed to break them.

On 27th October 1976 Stanisław Wijata wrote a complaint to the Public Prosecutors' Office. In it he has stated as follows: "I had been working in the Walter Works, in department P3. I was beaten up initially outside the factory, while being bundled into a black Volga car which was to take me to the police station. I was again beaten on my way there. During my period of detention I was made to run several times through the so-called "health-trots". During the interrogation I was made to stand with my face to the wall, while the police agents beat me with their truncheons, fists and keys. I have also been kicked."

On the 24th November 1976 Antoni Macierewicz, a member of the Workers' Defence Committee, received through the post a copy of a letter addressed to the Public Prosecutors' Office, withdrawing the above allegations:

"What I have said was untrue, because some people, saying they are from some Workers' Committee in Warsaw, wrote out the complaint for me and told me to sign it. I didn't even know what it was I was signing, but they told me it would be all right. Then they gave me two thousand zlotys".

What sort of a state does a man have to be driven to, to sign with his own hand a confession, that for two thousand zlotys he had lied by accusing and slandering the innocent police and security agents? Stanisław Wijata was broken.* No one can redress that wrong. Wijata's fate still hangs over all those who have dared to tell the truth. Only the pressure of a united public opinion can save them. Current attempts at intimidation and terror are designed to conceal the facts of beating and torture. Only by revealing the truth can such practices be made impossible.

On 15th November the Workers' Defence Committee appealed to the Polish Parliament to set up a Parliamentary Commission to study and make a public statement of the circumstances of the workers' strikes and demonstrations on 25th June 1976. This is not enough. We appeal for letters, petitions and resolutions requesting the setting up of a Parliamentary Commission to study and reveal all the circumstances of the June events.

Warsaw, 29th November 1976.

The Workers' Defence Committee
20 signatures follow.

Appeal of 34 Professors
To the Parliament
of the Polish People's Republic

Warsaw, 21st December 1976

We appeal to the Parliament of the Polish People's Republic to set up a Parliamentary Commission with the aim of undertaking a thorough and objective study of the workers' strikes and demonstrations of 25th June 1976 as well

---

* Ten days later Wijata re-affirmed his original complaint.

as the legal proceedings arising out of those events, the reprisals applied by both factory managements and the security authorities and of the activities of citizens in defence of workers who have been the targets of those reprisals.

It is generally accepted that the Court of Appeal's decision to reduce the terms of imprisonment of sentenced Ursus workers, who had been accused of sabotage, was influenced by the Polish Catholic Hierarchy's intervention. However, the full text of the Episcopate's appeal has never been made public by either the press or by any other mass-media. Similarly, the press, radio and television do not give any information about the activities of the Committee set up by a group of citizens to defend workers, who have been the victims of reprisals.

Lack of complete and honest information about the events of 25th June, as well as of their consequences, facilitates the circulation of rumours and deceitful information. This, in turn, increases unrest and arouses bitterness. We believe that only objective and detailed investigation of this affair by an authoritative body, such as a Parliamentary Commission, followed by publication of its findings — which the people have a right to demand — will stop the rising tide of discontent.

Prof. Franciszek Abramowicz, Chairman of Council of the Inst. of Physiology and Animal Husbandry, PAS;

Prof. Anatol Brzoza, Inst. of Agrarian Economy, Associate Member of the Polish Academy of Sciences (PAS);

Prof. Irena Chmielewska, Dept. of Biological Sciences, Member of the PAS;

Prof. Izydora Dąmbska, Inst. of Philosophy and Sociology, PAS;

Prof. Eugeniusz Domański, Inst. of Physiology, PAS; Ass. Member of PAS;

Prof. Andrzej Duda, Inst. of Maths., PAS;

Prof. Zbigniew Ryszard Grabowski, Inst. of Physical Chemistry, PAS;

Prof. Andrzej Grzegorczyk, Inst. of Philosophy and Sociology, PAS;

Prof. Stefan Gumiński, Inst. of Botanics, University of Wrocław;

130

Prof. Stanisław Hartman, Inst. of Maths., PAS;
Prof. Stanisław Hubert, Inst. of Constitutional Law, Wrocław University;
Prof. Wiktor Kemula, Inst. of Physical Chemistry, PAS; Member of PAS;
Prof. Jan Kielanowski, Institute of Physiology, PAS; Member of PAS;
Prof. Władysław Kunicki-Goldfinger, Inst. of Microbiology, Warsaw University, Member of PAS;
Prof. Halina Kurkowska, Inst. of Polish Philology, Warsaw University;
Prof. Józef Łukaszewicz, Inst. of Mathematics, Wrocław University;
Prof. Marian Malowist, Inst. of History, Warsaw University;
Prof. Irena Michalska, Inst. of Physiology and Animal Husbandry, PAS;
Prof. Włodzimierz Niemierko, Inst. of Experimental Biology, PAS, Member of PAS;
Prof. Stefan Nowak, Inst. of Sociology, Warsaw University;
Prof. Marian Nunberg, Dept. of Agronomy and Forestry, Member of PAS;
Prof. Czesław Pigoń, Director of the Inst. of Organic and Physical Chemistry, Wrocław Technical University;
Prof. Hanna Polaczkowa, Inst. of Chemistry and Organic Technology, Wrocław Technical University;
Prof. Anna Rudzka-Cybisowa, Academy of Fine Arts, Cracow;
Prof. Zofia Skrowaczewska, Inst. of Organic and Physical Chemistry, Wrocław
Prof. Marian Suski, Inst. of Telecomunications and Acoustics, Wrocław Technical University;
Prof. Stefan Świeżawski, Dept. of Philosophy, The Catholic University of Lublin;
Prof. Władysław Tomkiewicz, Dept. of History, Warsaw University;
Prof. Zbigniew Wierzbicki, Inst. of Philosophy and Sociology, PAS.
Prof. Zbigniew Wójcik, Inst. of History, PAS;
Prof. Kazimierz Zakrzewski, physician, Inst. of Nuclear Research, PAS;
Prof. Czesław Zgorzelski, Literary historian, The Catholic University of Lublin;

Prof. Tadeusz Zipser, Inst. of Architecture and Town Planning, Wrocław Technical University;
Prof. Grażyna Znaniecka, Inst. of Physiology, PAS.

Appeal of the 172 Intellectuals

Warsaw, 6th January 1977

To representatives of the world of culture and learning who are Members of the Sejm

Complaints and protests received from workers persecuted for having taken part in the June demonstrations make horrifying reading. They include reports of beatings after arrest and of torture during examination. Certain injuries sustained by the victims at that time have not healed to this day.

The Sejm has already received an appeal asking it to appoint a Commission to inquire into the abuses of law and the use of violence by the police as reported by the workers concerned. It is intolerable that persons under arrest should be subjected to maltreatment and torture. Every decent person has the moral and civil obligation to condemn and actively oppose these repugnant practices. Numerous centres of the intelligentsia have engaged in organising help, trying to stop the reprisals and prevent further persecution. Our hope is, however, limited. You, members of the Sejm, have wide prerogatives and are protected by parliamentary immunity. Your opportunities to act are much greater than ours and we appeal to you to use your influence on behalf of the victims of torture and violence.

We appeal to all the artists, writers and academics among the members of the Sejm: to Jarosław Iwaszkiewicz, the senior parliamentarian, to the Deputy President, the architect Halina Skibniewska, to the sociologist professor Jan Szczepański, to the actor Gustaw Holubek, to the novelist Wojciech Żukrowski, to the columnist Karol Małcużyński, to Ryszard Bender, professor of the Catholic University in Lublin, to the writer Tadeusz Hołuj, to Sylwester Zawadzki, professor of law, to the journalist Konstanty Łubieński, to the professors of medicine Henryk Rafalski and Halina Koźniewska, to the writers Bogdan Czeszko, Edmund Osmańczyk and Zbigniew Załuski, to the actor Mariusz Dmochowski, to Mieczysław Rakowski, editor of "Polityka" and to all other representatives of the country's cultural life who are members of the Sejm. The victims' accusations must not be received in silence. Silence in this case could only be construed as acquiescence to the abuse of law and a triumph of brute force. The whole country is aware of abuses, they are the subject of discussion everywhere and it is imperative that a Commission of Inquiry, consisting of members of the Sejm, be appointed to look into the accusations.

We hope that all those to whom we now appeal will take immediate measures leading to the establishment of the Commission.

Joanna Arnold — translator, Daria Andriejew — educationalist, Wojciech Arkuszewski — physicist, Władysław Bartoszewski — historian and journalist, Jolanta Maurin-Białostocka — art historian, Konrad Bieliński — mathematician, Jacek Bocheński — writer, Teresa Bogucka — sociologist, Seweryn Blumsztajn — sociologist, Andrzej Braun — writer, Bogusława Blajfer, Przemysław Bystrzycki — writer, Kazimierz Brandys — writer, Marian Brandy — writer, Tomasz Burek — writer, Barbara Bozym — philologist, Andrzej Bieńkowski — artist, Ewa Bieńkowska — Romance studies, Małgorzata Braunek — actress, Andrzej Bełczyński — lawyer, Maksymilian Boratyński — mathematician, Stefan Boratyński — lawyer, Bogdan Chwedeńczuk — editor, Andrzej Celiński — sociologist, Józef Chajn — chemist, Maria Dziewicka — historian, Jan Dziendziora — painter, Andrzej Drawicz — writer, Stanisław Drozd — psychologist, Jerzy Ficowski — writer, Kazimierz Frieske — socjologist, Piotr Fronczewski — actor, Jan Gadomski — economist, Anna Górecka — architect, Agnieszka Grudzińska — philologist, Mieczysław Grudziński — engineer, Roman Gren — biologist, Renata Grzegorczyk — philologist, Joanna Guze — writer and translator, Jolanta Grzegorek — journalist, Marek Grzesiński — Polish studies, Jacek Gąsiorowski — Polish studies, Włodzimierz Gromiec — philosopher, Helena Zofia Gromiec — editor, Janusz Górski-Bratczuk, Helena Hagemajerowa — economist, Krzysztof Herbts — sociologist, Hanna Igalson — translator, Zofia Jasińska — theatre historian, Andrzej Jastrzębski — editor, Joanna Justyna Janeczek — journalist, Janina Kaczanowska — biolog, Anna Kamieńska —

writer, Jadwiga Komorowska — sociologist, Marek Kondrat — actor, Zygmunt Komorowski — sociologist, Anna Kowalska — writer, Jacek Kleyff — satirist, Wojciech Kochlewski — engineer, Jan Krzysztof Kelus — sociologist, Zofia Kuzelanka — editor, Maria Kosińska — art historian, Marek Kesy — sociollogist, Kesy — physicist, Roman Kornecki — journalist, Grażyna Borucka Kuroń — psychologist, Aleksandra Korejwa — producer, Tadeusz Konwicki — writer, Andrzej Kijowski — writer, Ryszard Krynicki — writer, Sławomir Kretkowski — historian, Kazimierz Kaczor — actor, Konstanty Jan Kurman — automation engineer, Waldemar Kuczyński — economist, Grażyna Kopińska — philologist, Maria Korniłowicz — writer, Olga Kersten — psychologist, Krzysztof Lant — chemist, Edward Lipski — information scientist, Antoni Libera — literary critic, Jan Lityński — mathematician, Maria Łoś — philosopher, Zdzisław Łapiński — critic, Małgorzata Łukasiewicz — translator, Andrzej Łodyński — philosopher, Hanna Malewska — writer, Aniela Makarewicz — biologist, Hanna Magnuska — sociologist, Janusz Mrozik — information scientist, Hanna Morawska — art historian, Anna Morawska — sociologist, Janusz Maciejewski — literary critic, Bogdan Matuszewski — biologist, Stefan Morawski — professor of aesthetics, Elżbieta Malicka — chemist, Ewa Milde — actress, Jerzy Markuszewski — producer, Zdzisław Mrózewski — actor, Irena Mazurek — philosopher, Mieczysław Mazurek — chemist, Natalia Modzelewska — writer, Marek Nowakowski — writer, Jerzy Narbutt — writer, Maria Hiszpańska-Neumann — artist, Wiktor Nagórski — information scientist, Wiktor Niedźwiedzki — philosopher, Daniel Olbrychski — actor, Wojciech Onyszkiewicz — historian, Jan Popiel — information scientist, Jadwiga Puzynina — philologist, Seweryn Pollak — writer, Anna Pogonowska — writer, Janusz Przewłocki — editor, Jan Prokop — critic, Ryszard Perryt — actor, Małgorzata Piotrowska — biologist, Aldona Pobojewska — philosopher, Sylwia Perryt, Michał Ryszkiewicz — mathematician, Hanna Rozner — philologist, Maciej Rajzacher — actor, Zofia Domaszewska — physicist, Zbigniew Romaszewski — physicist, Wincenty Rutkiewicz — architect, Ewa Rose-Boratyńska — doctor, Ewa Strzeszewska — psychologist, Jan Staszeli — mathematician, Tadeusz Szawiel — sociologist, Jadwiga Sambor — philologist, Joanna Szczęsna — philologist, Eugenia Siemaszkiewicz —

writer, Małgorzata Szpakowska — critic, Adam Szymanowski — translator, Krystyna Starczewska — philosopher, Andrzej Seweryn — actor, Hanna Skarżanka — actress, Barbara Stepniewska-Holzer — historian, Józef Stanosz — computer scientist, Zofia Kossakowska-Szanojca — art historian, Mirosława Suska — historian, Stefania Stopnicka — editor, Urszula Sikorska — sociologist, Andrzej Szarkowski — sociologist, Irena Topińska — economist, Barbara Toruńczyk — sociologist, Krzysztof Turalski — philologist, Andrzej Tyszka — sociologist, Krzysztof Wagner — information scientist, Wiktor Woroszylski — writer, Adam Wojciechowski — lawyer, Janusz Węgielek — writer, Wanda Wagner — physicist, Maria Wosiek — theatre historian, Kazimierz Wójcicki — journalist, Janusz Weiss — satirist, Barbara Wrzesińska — actress, Jan Wyka — writer, Janusz Wiśniewski — graphic artist, Joanna Walter — writer and translator, Włodzimierz Witaszewski — architect, Jan Walc — journalist, Grażyna Kubicka-Weiss — Polish studies, Maria Zagórska — translator, Adam Zagajewski — writer, Zbigniew Zawadzki — chemist, Barbara Zbrożyna — sculptor, Piotr Zaborowski — actor, Krzysztof Zaleski — Polish studies, Ewa Żółkiewska — Romance studies, Krystyna Żeglarska — psychologist. (172 signatures)

Letter of the 185 priests of the Przemyśl Diocese
Przemyśl, 25th January 1977

To Mr. Stanisław Gucwa,
The President of the Sejm,
Polish People's Republic.

Dear Mr. President,
On behalf of our parishioners, we the undersigned priests appeal to you, Mr. President, to propose a motion at the next plenary session of the Sejm resolving that a Special Parliamentary Commission be set up to investigate impartially the allegations of police brutality during the events of last June in Ursus and Radom. The matter has acquired particular urgency following the Chief Public Prosecutors' statement to the Sejm Commission for Home Affairs and Justice on 5th January 1977 on the subject of the professional conduct of the police and security services in Ursus and Radom last June. We are under the impression that our supreme authorities are not adequately informed of the current developments

in the economic and socio-political life of the country. As citizens of the Polish People's Republic we are entitled to apply to you, Mr. President, to place this motion before the Sejm Commission for Home Affairs and Justice and subsequently at the plenary session of the Sejm.

OPEN LETTER OF WARSAW UNIVERSITY STUDENTS

To Stanisław Gucwa, the President of the Sejm, for consideration by the Sejm.

The Council of State has decided, on the recommendation of the First Secretary of the Polish United Workers' Party, to exercise clemency in regard to certain people sentenced as a result of the events of 25th June 1976. This indicates that the authorities wish to alleviate the tensions created by the events and their aftermath.

Public anxiety cannot, however, be assuaged until allegations are investigated that the authorities infringed on the human rights of workers who were involved in the disturbances. We therefore request that the Sejm should appoint an Extraordinary Parliamentary Commission to inquire into allegations: that the workers detained in Radom and Ursus were subjected to police brutality, being repeatedly beaten until they fell unconscious and/or ordered to run the gauntlet between two rows of policemen; that these methods were used for the purpose of extracting false statements from the detainees; and, that many of the workers lost their jobs because they took part in the strikes.

The institutions responsible for maintaining the rule of law must be made accountable for their actions and the public must be reassured that the widely ranging powers of those institutions will not be abused. The conduct of the police, the Public Prosecutors' Office, the courts and the industrial managements involved in the aftermath of the June events should all come under the scrutiny of the Commission.

The confidence that there is no likelihood of these methods being used again, shall only be restored if this be done.

We shall make the contents of this letter public.

On 9th March 1977 the above Letter, signed by 730 students of Warsaw University, was delivered to the Sejm offices by a delegation consisting of: Jan Ajzner, 4th year, Dept. of Sociology; Jan Cywiński, 2nd year, Dept. of Classical Philology; Marcin Gogulski, 1st year, Dept. of Mathematics and Mechanics; Stefan Kawalec, 4th year, Dept. of Mathematics and Mechanics; Sergiusz Kowalski, 5th year, Dept. of Mathematics and Mechanics; Paweł Nassalski, 3rd year, Dept. of Sociology; Anna Pełka, 4th year, Institute of Social Prophilactics and Rehabilitation; Jadwiga Prokop, 5th year, Dept. of Psychology; Ewa Tarasiewicz, 4th year, Dept. of Psychology; Hanna Turczyn, 3rd year, Dept. of Mathematics and Mechanics.

AMNESTY?

THE WORKERS' DEFENCE COMMITTEE

STATEMENT

Warsaw, 5th February 1977

On 3rd February 1977 the Council of State, on the recommendation of the First Secretary of the Party, instructed the Sentence Review Commission, the Chief Public Prosecutor's Office and other bodies entrusted with the administration of justice "to prepare proposals for the reprieve, the reduction of sentences and suspension of the remaining portion of the sentences being served; this to apply to prisoners sentenced in connection with the June events who have shown repentance and are unlikely to revert to crime".

We greet the decision of the Council of State as a first step towards repairing the injustice done to those who took part in the June protest. The joy felt at the prospect of their release must not, however, blind us to the fundamental flaws in the Council's resolution. It is accompanied by the anxiety caused by the news that the Council of State approved the reports of the Chief Public Prosecutor, the Chairman of the Supreme Court and the Minister of Justice regarding the conduct of their departments and the services for which they are responsible during and following the June events.

If the reprieves and suspensions are to apply only to those who "have shown repentance and are unlikely to revert to crime" we must point out that this exercise of clemency would presuppose an act of self-humiliation on the part of the prisoners and it would exclude those still intent on defending the rights of workers and their own dignity.

It would not apply to those who simply feel innocent, nor those who were brutally treated and who, surely, have the right to expect repentance from the men responsible for their sufferings. Whatever the intentions of the First Secretary, the Council of State's resolution gives the very people in whose interests it is to conceal the abuses committed, an added power over the prisoners whose release would depend on them.

The Workers' Defence Committee will seek to inform the public about the manner in which the resolution of the Council of State is implemented.

Promises contained in the Council's resolution provide additional grounds for public anxiety since they are associated with an expression of approval for the past conduct of the security services and the judiciary, who, allegedly, "reduced the punishment and recommended suspension of sentences generously and with understanding".

The Workers' Defence Committee consider it their duty to list a number of relevant facts.

On 31st January the most recent appeal case of the Radom workers was heard by the Supreme Court. In all the trials in the series, the defendants were charged under article 275 for taking part in an unlawful assembly and not, as the official reports proclaimed, for larceny and theft. Nevertheless, the sentences were as much as ten years. The verdicts and sentences of the Supreme Court represent a dangerous precedent with wide social implications. The principle of collective responsibility was applied by the Court: each of the accused was made responsible for the injuries suffered by all the 75 policemen and for the total cost of the damage, amounting, allegedly, to 28 million zlotys. It is horrifying to hear the Supreme Court ruling, for political reasons, that, as the accused "had no reasonable grounds for protest", their behaviour merited charges of hooliganism, an offence carrying incidentally a much higher sentence. The precedent, thus established, of combining article 275 (unlawful assembly) and 59 (hooliganism) in the charge, will make it possible for the courts in the future to treat all the workers' demonstrations as hooligan excesses.

The Supreme Court demonstrated a lack of objectivity by accepting, without exception, all the police evidence given by the prosecution. What the Court accepted included the evidence of a witness who, at different hearings, ascribed the same action to different defendants, and of another who gave evidence concerning events which occurred simultaneously in different parts of the town. Majak, Opolski and a number of others gave evidence of that kind. The Court did not admit any of the defendants' evidence concerned with torture, beating, statements taken under duress and other forms of brutality during questioning.

The Supreme Court made no effort to examine the strange circumstances in which looting occurred in Radom. According to our information, when the demonstrations were over, a small close-knit group of people appeared in the centre of the town and systematically broke all the shop windows. This led to looting and smash-and-grab raids, later to be blamed on the demonstrators. It is also to be noted that the courts, while treating the demonstrators with the utmost severity dealt mildly with those indicted for robbery and looting; these, as a rule, were given suspended sentences. The demonstrators were made to bear responsibility not only for their own actions but for the occurrences throughout the town and for worker protests throughout the country. Their own particular particle of responsibility was of so little importance to the Court that it was not even considered necessary for it to be proved.

Even if, for the sake of argument, we were to assume that the defendants committed all the offences with which they were charged, the severity of the sentences would still appear remarkable. For instance, Jan Sadowski, a father of three, "having entered the Party building with the crowd, used improper language, encouraged others to damage public property, broke doors and windows, desks and chairs", was sentenced to 5 years' imprisonment. Bogdan Borkowicz, 22, "threw stones at the Party building, broke several windows, used improper language and loudly encouraged others to damage the building", sentenced to 6 years' imprisonment. Ryszard Grudzień "lead a group of people engaged in throwing stones, encouraged the whole crowd to follow their example and, with others, damaged the furnishings in the Party building" was sentenced to 9 years. The above are quoted from the Supreme Court's judgement.

The charges had not been proved but this did not prevent the verdicts being passed, and inordinately long sentences imposed. Following these decisions of the Supreme Court, no one in this country can feel safe. Merely to stand by, however, and remain silent in the face of this grotesque illegality, thinly disguised by the majesty of the law, is to become both a part of the conspiracy as well as its potential victim.

There is no question of justice in a situation in which the accused are in fact hostages. A court sentence should be distinguishable from the retribution wrought by a distracted owner, saddened at the loss of his possessions.

Seven months after the June events, the First Secretary discussed his recommendations to the Council of State at a meeting attended by a few hundred Party activists at Ursus. A few weeks earlier, 1,100 Ursus workers* petitioned the First Secretary to reinstate in their old jobs all the workers sacked as a result of the June events. The First Secretary has not acknowledged receipt of this petition.

Yet, following the June protests there had been mass sackings throughout the country. The Workers' Defence Committee reiterates the workers' demands:

All those dismissed should be reinstated without a break in continuity of employment and without loss of occupational and social rights acquired prior to dismissal.

There should be an unconditional amnesty for all those detained and sentenced for their part in the June protests.

The full scale of the post-June reprisals and the surrounding circumstances should be made public.

Those guilty of breaking the law, of torture and brutality should be brought to trial and publicly condemned.

The Workers' Defence Committee demands the appointment of a Parliamentary Commission to conduct an unbiased inquiry into the grave and harrowing problems of the situation.

When these demands are met, the need for the existence of the Workers' Defence Committee will be at an end.

There follow 23 signatures

---

* Originally 889 workers signed this petition (p. 112). When the Security Service tried to induce workers to withdraw their signatures, a further 211 added theirs, both as a mark of solidarity with the 889 and the WDC and also as a protest against the behaviour of the authorities.

140

Chomicki, who remained behind bars despite hunger-strikes and protests on his behalf, and similarly Majewski, Żukowski and Maciejczyk whose prison sentences were upheld in March were a constant reminder that the amnesty was selective.

THE MURDER OF PYJAS AND
THE COMMITTEE FOR STUDENT SOLIDARITY

The Workers' Defence Committee has had a large measure of support from university students (the fact that over 1,600 students petitioned Parliament is ample indication). One of its leading supporters in Cracow, Poland's second largest city, was Stanisław Pyjas a student in his final year at the Jagiellonian University. On Saturday 7 May his body was found in the doorway of a block of flats with his head battered in. The authorities maintain that his fatal injuries were sustained as a result of a fall down a flight of stairs while under the influence of alcohol — the autopsy stated that he had drunk the equivalent of half a litre of vodka.

However, even a superficial study of the facts showed glaring inconsistencies. He was found at 7.20 a.m. (the time of death was put at 3.00 a.m.) but people would be leaving for work from 6.00 a.m. onwards. Moreover his body was discovered some distance away from the nearest stairs. Furthermore he had been the subject of a campaign of denigration: five of his friends had received anonymous letters on 19 and 20 April insinuating that he was a police informer and inciting them to "settle matters with this nasty character once and for all by any possible means at your disposal".

The Requiem Mass for Pyjas was attended by some 2000 students who formed a procession after the service and marched across the city's main square to the place where his body was found. A boycott, almost wholly successful, was then declared of the annual student rag for the week-end following the funeral.

As a result of the death and subsequent behaviour of the official student organizations, a Committee for Student Solidarity was set up in Cracow with the aim of representing the genuine interests of the students. In their first declaration, the CSS called for thorough investigation into all the aspects of the death of Pyjas.

Cracow, 15th May, 1977

THE COMMITTEE FOR
STUDENT SOLIDARITY IN CRACOW
DECLARATION

On 7th May our friend, Stanisław Pyjas, a student of Philology and Philosophy at the Jagiellonian University, died tragically in mysterious circumstances.

The deceased was a person who held independent and non-conformist views. In the last phase of his life he actively co-operated with the Workers' Defence Committee. His death left a deep-felt sense of shock among the academic community, not only in Cracow but throughout the country. The Workers' Defence Committee made an official protest, circulated in their statement of May 9th.

The students of Cracow have spontaneously responded to this shocking act of murder by deciding to boycott all the events of the traditional annual festivities [rag]. Neither the students nor the inhabitants of Cracow were left to mourn Stanisław's death undisturbed, for they were harassed by officials of the Security Services. Many of our colleagues who went to mourn were detained and arrested and even the place of mourning was frequently desecrated. In this way the Socialist Students' Union has lost the ultimate moral right of representing the academic community. Thus on May 15th we called together the Committee for Student Solidarity in order to initiate the forming of an authentic and independent student

The Committee for Student Solidarity states that the circumstances surrounding the death of Stanisław Pyjas require a public explanation by qualified representatives of the authorities and that those guilty of the crime must be brought to justice regardless of the positions they hold.

The Committee for Student Solidarity demands an explanation of the circumstances surrounding the acts of profanity at the place where Stanisław Pyjas was mourned and demands that those guilty of such acts be punished.

The Committee appeals to all for support and for information about the victimization of those who took part in the mourning ceremonies. We hereby state that we wish to organize ourselves in self-defence against reprisals.

The Committee for Student Solidarity allies itself with the Workers' Defence Committee.

The members of the Committee for Student Solidarity authorize the following people to represent the standpoint of the Committee for Student Solidarity: 1. Lesław *Maleszka*, 2. Andrzej *Balcerek*, 3. Lilianna *Batko*, 4. Elżbieta *Majewska*, 5. Małgorzata *Gatkiewicz*, 6. Wiesław *Bek*, 7. Bogumił *Fonik*, 8. Joanna *Barczyk*, 9. Bronisław *Wildstein*, 10. Robert *Kaczmarek*, 11. Katarzyna *Ptak*, 12. Józef *Roszar*.

142

HARASSMENT OF THE WDC AND
THE BUREAU FOR INTERVENTIONS

The murder of Pyjas marks a particularly fearsome point in a history of mounting harassment of WDC members and their collaborators. Another example is provided by Wojciech Onyszkiewicz, who on his way back from Cracow, after attending Pyjas' funeral, was involved in a serious car accident which had been contrived by the security forces. In this situation of growing persecution the WDC formed a Bureau for Interventions to deal with acts of lawlessness and violations of human and civil rights by recording them and organizing aid where possible. The WDC thereby extended its scope of action.

The harassment of Committee members has taken various forms. On all but one occasion when members attended court hearings in Radom, they were afterwards detained for questioning often long into the night. In the course of this they have, some of them, been insulted, threatened and beaten up. They have been assaulted even within the precincts of the Court buildings. Two members, Macierewicz and Chojecki, were dismissed from their academic posts. Others have faced trumped-up charges: Puzyna was accused of breaking into a street kiosk in Warsaw despite an obvious alibi — he was away in Radom attending a trial. (One might wonder whether such a police need be feared. However, it is a sad reflection on Poland's judicial system that Puzyna might have been tried and almost certainly convicted.) Halina Mikołajska, the eminent actress, was accused of stealing a sheepskin coat from a fellow passenger on the train. Zdziarski was taken from his home and, after questioning, abandoned in a forest. Appartments are frequently searched and food and money destined for workers, confiscated. Threatening 'phone-calls, deflated car tyres, cut brake-cables — these and many others are the order of the day. More recently, having been several times detained for the statutory maximum of 48 hours without charge, six members and a number of helpers were held from 15 May for an unspecified period under the terms of "Prosecutor's sanction". They were released by the amnesty of 22nd July 1977.

The following document relates some of the harassment and justifies the founding of the Bureau for Interventions.

THE WORKERS' DEFENCE COMMITTEE

Warsaw, 10th May, 1977

DECLARATION

The Workers' Defence Committee considers it its duty to inform the public about the growing rate of criminal behaviour as practised by the authorities in our country. In our statement concerning the tragic death of Stanisław Pyjas we issued information showing how physical acts of terror were inflicted

143

on those who associate themselves with the Workers' Defence Committee. Alongside these incidents the persecution and humiliation of individuals for their activities within the community and for their political beliefs is growing dangerously frequent, those who joined the Workers' Defence Committee to organize aid for the victims of the June reprisals and those who signed letters addressed to the Sejm (Parliament) demanding the appointment of a special Parliamentary Committee are now themselves severely victimized.

During the past few months S. Blumsztajn, M. Chojecki, J. Lityński, A. Macierewicz, J. Szczęsna and W. Ziembiński, who had all been associated with the Workers' Defence Committee, lost their jobs. Until recently employers still sought pretences for dismissal. In the last while, however, the situation has undergone a marked change. Pretences are no longer necessary, social views and political beliefs now constitute an explicit reason either for dismissal or for organizing a persecution campaign. Andrzej Celiński was dismissed from his post at Warsaw University for his political beliefs. The Regional Committee of Recall justified his dismissal with these words: "In a private conversation with the Secretary of the Works Committee, A. Kałużyński, A. Celiński mentioned his views concerning the June events in Radom and at Ursus." The Managing Board and the party leadership of the Electrical and Engineering Institute in Warsaw unleashed a persecution campaign, very reminiscent of the psychological terrors of the Stalinist era, against five of its employees (Dr. A. Głowacki, Engineer S. Klimek, Engineer M. Kociszewska-Szczerbik, Dr. A. Wołyński, Dr. R. Zdrojewski), who had added their signatures to an appeal addressed to the Polish Sejm. They are now being called for talks — interrogations; ordered to revoke their letter to the Sejm, in writing; their colleagues have been incited against them; a demand has been made for the dismissal of a member of the Works Committee who added his signature to the letter; public meetings, condemning them outright, are being organized within the Institute (the editor, M. Misiorny was invited to take an active part in one of these); resolutions are being passed against them by listing the names of all those attending the meeting instead of the names of the voters. Those who signed the letter to the Polish Sejm stand accused of acts of sabotage and of allying themselves with enemy groups in the West, hostile to Poland; colleagues who added their signatures to the letter and who argue against the stand taken by the Managing Board and the Party leadership of the Electrical and Engineering Institute are being persecuted and terrorised. Some of those most acti-' vely involved in this persecution campaign are: the director of the Electrical and Engineering Institute, W. Seruga, the chief specialist for works' affairs and secretary of Party organization, R. Łojek together with T. Cesul, Z. Kajczyński, H. Szumiejko, H. Zagórski, E. Zasada. A more detailed account of this campaign will be reported in the Information Bulletin. Similar methods of persecution against those who ally themselves with the Workers' Defence Committee have been started in other establishments.

In March, April and May of this year, officials of the , Security Services raided private homes in Warsaw, Łódź, Cracow and Poznań, checking on Workers' Defence Committee members and sympathisers, searching them and detaining them for many hours of questioning, taking photographs and fingerprints. A dozen or more were detained for 48 hours. All of them were called for questioning at the Public Prosecutor's Office. The daughters, who are still minors, of Władysław Sulecki, a miner from the "Gliwice" colliery, co-operating with ' the Workers' Defence Committee, were interrogated by the Security Services and incited to inform on their father. We know of other, similar cases. These are only a few examples of the authorities' criminal behaviour and of their violent disregard for and violation of human rights. It is an extremely grave and serious situation, one that we must not underestimate. We must not overlook its incalculable consequences. We have to oppose it with all our might and as actively as possible. We appeal to every single individual to act at all times to oppose any act of terror and persecution, whether it be directed against his fellow citizens, his colleagues or against himself, and whether it takes place at work, in his professional or social environment, or in his union. Solidarity is now an absolute necessity and self-defence by the community as a whole is indispensable. Every violation of human rights and of our rights as citizens, which goes uncensored, which passes without opposition and without being brought before the public eye will eventually severely injure every

10*   145

one of us, though it may not, at that moment, be aimed at us. Every infringement that passes without comment becomes an antecedent to another transgression. We become accomplices to every violation that we let pass in silence.

In this situation, where acts of lawlessness are growing in number, the Workers' Defence Committee acknowledges the necessity for appointing a Bureau of Intervention. Its function will be to collect evidence of any violation of human and citizens' rights and then to inform the public. Whenever it lies within its power to do so it will try to give legal aid where possible, medical aid where needed and financial aid where absolutely necessary to the victims of unjust treatment by establishments of work, by trade unions, by the administrative organs of the State, by the Security Services or by the judiciary. It also becomes necessary to form a Fund for the Self-Defence of the Community in order to establish continuing aid for victims of reprisals and of criminal behaviour by the authorities. This Fund will be instituted directly after the accounts of the Workers' Defence Committee have been cleared. We call on the following people to help set out the principles of administering the Fund: Prof. Jan Kielanowski, Prof. Edward Lipiński, Dr. Jan Józef Lipski, Dr. Józef Rybicki, Halina Mikołajska, Wacław Zawadzki, Rev. Jan Zieja.

The Workers' Defence Committee appeals to all citizens to oppose any manifest act of criminal behaviour. We call on individuals to relay every reliable piece of information concerning known cases of violation of the law by the authorities. The Workers' Defence Committee wishes to stress its conviction that widespread and purposeful action by a united community is the only way to counteract acts of violence, and to check the recurring violations of human and citizens' rights which are being committed with such impunity in our country. We alone, with justice to support us, can fight against injustice.

The Workers' Defence Commitee

(24 signatures follow)

Chapter six

THE CATHOLIC CHURCH

The Role of the Church in Poland

A close link has always existed in Poland between the Catholic Church and the people. Both have shared the same fate for centuries — more than 3,000 priests, almost a third of their total, were killed in World War 2, some losing their lives in concentration camps. Today some 90% of the population regard themselves as Catholics, members of a body which presents an alternative and independent set of values in a one-party state. It is for this reason that the Communist authorities have always proceeded very warily in their relations with the Church. Their tactics have varied according to their strength at a particular moment.

In the immediate post-war period, the Party felt that it was not yet strong enough to challenge an institution which had such a hold on the vast majority of the population. Thus Party leaders were to be seen walking in religious processions and all great State occasions began with Mass at the Warsaw Cathedral.

However, once the Communists had achieved complete political control, relations deteriorated steadily. In September 1953, the Primate, Cardinal Stefan Wyszyński, was placed under house arrest in an isolated monastery in the Bieszczady Mountains in the South of Poland. By the end of the same year eight bishops and 900 priests were in prison. Religious instruction was forbidden in schools and official permission for the building of new churches became almost impossible to obtain.

Relations changed fundamentally when Władysław Gomułka returned to power in October 1956. (In times of crisis, the Communists have always held out the hand of friendship to the Church.) This was symbolised by the Church-State agreement of December 1956 which, inter alia, saw the incorporation of religious education into the school time-table. The Catholic Church has always insisted that the children of believers have a right to religious instruction irrespective of the prevailing political ideology. The Polish Communists cannot, of course, be expected to help propagate a philosophy which stands in direct contradiction to their own materialistic and dialectic approach. The question of religious education should therefore be seen as one of the litmus tests as to the true nature of Church-State relations in Poland.

The high hopes of 1956 began to dissipate quite quickly. Permission to build churches — especially in those new areas which had been developed after the war, again became difficult to obtain. In July 1961 religious education within the schools was made illegal.

All this was part of a general political clamp-down as the authorities tried to withdraw those relaxations which they had originally allowed in an effort to consolidate support. A one-party state cannot allow any long term genuine relaxations — otherwise, sooner or later, its own basis of power will be questioned. But as the authorities become increasingly divorced from the aspirations of society, the danger looms larger and larger that a decision might be made which will be violently rejected by important groups in the population — there being no other way open to them for expressing their opinions, as all the normal channels of communication and expression are in the Party's total control.

This is precisely what happened in December 1970, when Gomułka wanted to increase the price of basic foods by about 25% without any corresponding increases in wages and salaries. The massive and violent revolt which erupted, toppled the leadership and Edward Gierek became Party chief. Again, one of the first acts of the new rulers was an appeal to the Church for support. Again there was a thaw in Church-State relations. And again they deteriorated within a few years. Once more it was a question of religious education.

In 1973 two official reports were published — one on the present state of education, the other on the duties of the State with regard to the upbringing of young people. Both documents stressed the need for a unified educational system designed to prepare its recipients for life in a "socialist" Poland. The school timetable was to be programmed in such a way that it would be physically impossible for children to receive religious instruction in a church. The Hierarchy responded by saying that "such intentions could deny a person his fundamental right to freedom of conscience and religion which are guaranteed in the Polish Constitution. State laws cannot be contrary to God's law otherwise they are not binding."

In May 1976, the Minister for Religious Affairs, Kazimierz Kąkol, made a speech to a group of trusted Party activists. It was a statement of Party views on religion whose contents were somehow leaked to the West. The following quotation speaks for itself.

"Even though, as a Minister, I have to smile to gain its [the Church's] confidence, as a Communist, I will fight it unceasingly both on an ideological and on a philosophical level. I feel ashamed when Communists from other countries ask me why so many Poles go to Church; I feel ashamed when guests congratulate me on the spread of religion in this country. Normalization of relations with the Church is not a capitulation. We will not make any compromises with the Church. It has the right to carry out its observances only within the confines of a sanctuary. We will never allow it to extend its evangelical activities outside those walls. We will never permit the religious up-

bringing of children. If we cannot destroy the Church, at least let us
stop it from causing harm."

The Church is now widely appreciated by intellectuals of all outlooks for its integrity in sustaining moral and intellectual resistance.
I* tries to promote ethical values in a system which encourages egotism
and corruption, and truth in a system based essentially on lies and deceit.
It enunciates a philosophy based on humanitarian principles, which
tries to encompass all aspects of life and thus all its problems.
Christianity is thus not purely a matter of worship — which the Communists would like to see confined strictly to church premises — but
a question of human relationships and a recognition of the real needs
of people and the way in which the people can be helped. Thus, in view
of the moral authority of the Church in Poland, the firm support
given at specific instances by the Hierarchy and Cardinal Wyszyński
himself to protests by intellectuals, workers and others ought to be
seen not so much as an additional voice of dissent, but as an authoritative '
endorsement, vouching for the morality and sincerity of those protests.*

THE CHURCH IN JUNE 1976 AND AFTER

Politics and religion

*The Church pulpit, unique as a source of the uncensored word,
has long been the mouthpiece for a voice eminently concerned for the
well-being, material and non-material alike, of the people of Poland.
The present sections give details of a number of Church documents,
Episcopal letters, memoranda drawn up by the Polish Hierarchy at
their sessional conferences and also excerpts from sermons and addresses by the Primate, Cardinal Stefan Wyszyński. These may suggest
at first sight that the Church assumes a dual role. For, on the one hand,
the documents bear witness to the Church's continual struggle against '
demoralization of society and to its fight for religious freedom, for the right
tc evangelize, to build new churches where they are needed, to publish.
On the other hand, they record a most outspoken and wide-ranging
concern for the welfare of the country, concern about the economy '
(in particular that the home market in foodstuffs receives a fair share
of produce with priority over export), the decline in the birth rate and
consequent future drop in population growth, agricultural reform (small
wonder in view of the Church's deep ties with the peasant community).
the conditions of work, public education, preservation of the environment. It would be wrong, however, to jump to the conclusion that this
second role amounts to abrogation of political competences. A resolution of the dual role is to be found in these words from the Primate's
sermon on Corpus Christi (17 June 1976):*

"There is no greater value that can enter into the life of
the nation, into the life of our religion, into the life of our
society than the very marriage of the affairs of God with
the affairs of Man."

It is important to see precisely this value as motivating the Church's role of what one might call an articulate conscience of Poland. This role does not spring from "political" aspiration (as naturally it might, say, in the case of political parties in the West); later that year (in his Christmas Day Sermon) *the Primate was at pains to point out this distinction, in view especially of the Church's outspoken championship of the workers' cause:*

"... let no one think that the Bishops embarked on a struggle against the system. No, they only recalled the rights of Man, of the family and citizens in their country. These are the only objectives that guide us. We cannot accept comments, appearing in particular in the foreign press, which scent political motives in everything we do. We are concerned with life, with the life of Man, the nation, the family, in the spirit of God's peace. These are the true motives guiding the Polish Bishops and priests in their toil. We do everything in our power that our country may be calmer, better, quieter, so that weeping shall not be heard, so that no one shall be beaten up, persecuted or ill-treated, so that police truncheons may be returned to store, so that everyone may feel secure, peaceful and respected in his native home. This requires much goodwill and the co-operation of us all... We should not be discouraged by anything, by any difficulties and obstacles, not even by wrongs inflicted upon us and we should resume work..."

In the context of this distinction, a useful insight may be gained by recalling how the Church attended to a long-term national interest of quite a different calibre. In 1965 the Polish Episcopate sought to bring about reconciliation between the Polish and the German nations by forgiving and asking to be forgiven the wrongs suffered and the retaliatory wrongs inflicted and by inviting dialogue between the Catholic Churches of both nations. This was a far-sighted policy (wholly in the spirit of the Second Vatican Council) aimed at future peace for the nation and opposed to the still current communist policy of stirring up old hatreds.

One cannot help noticing that the message of brotherly love and dignity transpiring through the Church's social programme and impinging even on the ecological issue, if it does not tender hope, must at the very least strike a truly harsh dissonance with those realities of every-day life which in June '76 drove the workers to acts of despair.

June 1976 and after

In the aftermath of June '76 the Church Hierarchy openly championed the cause of oppressed workers. They appealed to the authorities, they reasoned with them, they sought the root causes of unrest, tracing disorder to a policy preoccupied with "saving" the rest of the world, (Third World and unfavourable exports to the Soviet Union, presumably were meant) at a time when the country was in need. They argued that peace, order and economic efficiency could be restored only by winning the confidence of the people and that the only way to achieve this was to respect Man, his labour and his civil rights. On the other hand, they encouraged the people to bring financial help to families of the oppressed workers.

Do the authorities generally appreciate the Church's advice? It is difficult to say, but it is interesting to note the following extract from an address by Kąkol (minister responsible for Church affairs) when he pledged himself to an all out fight against the Church at a meeting of activists and trusted pressmen in May 1976 (see page 148):

"Lately we have exercised ourselves in the epistolary art. That is the current fashion. The Bishops never stop writing. We are snowed under by their memoranda (their letters are variously styled) which raise all kinds of problems, such as the right to work, the merging of the youth organizations, etc. There was one even on folk culture and even one — as you will know — on the Constitution.

We reply civilly, as is due, when someone writes to us; but how can one reply intelligently to stupid letters?"

Letter to the authorities on behalf of the workers

On July 16th the Polish Episcopate appealed to the authorities on behalf of the workers. In their letter they declared that it was a disparagment to the workers to connect their justified protest against excessive price increases on foodstuffs with the acts of violence which had been committed at the time by a few disreputable individuals; further, that the prison sentences, which ran to over three years, were too harsh. They stated that it was unjust to dismiss workers when they had demonstrated and had struck to defend themselves and their families against the exorbitant increases which had been the misdoing of the authorities. Part of the blame for the demonstrations and unrest lay with the authorities and the trade unions which had not properly informed the Party leadership.

On the economy

' On 15th August 1976 (the feast of the Assumption) the Primate turned his attention to the food shortages in a sermon to 20,000 pilgrims at Częstochowa. He said that "feeding the people of this country should be the first priority, only then may food exports be considered."

He was to expand this view on the economy in a Christmas address to the clergy of Warsaw:

"... Surely the materialistic system, asserting as it does the primacy of matter, ought to have reaped the best results, yet the facts of reality deny this, though one is not so much as allowed to mention the so-called crisis. The day before yesterday, when I was returning from Gniezno to Warsaw, everywhere along the way I saw in many towns unending queues in front of the shops, of women, children, overworked men, shivering in the cold. Yet in Parliament the word "crisis" may not be spoken, for that is an activity that might create the impression of crisis — as though it needed still to be produced, as though it did not yet exist.

How then are we to explain these painful symptoms, so humiliating to an industriously working nation? A tactful mention in Parliament of our economic difficulties evoked the reply that they were all the doing of forces hostile to the People's Republic. Are then these women and children who queue for a piece of meat or bread, the enemies of People's Poland? Did they even dream of taking any action against Poland or the system? Or is it — as was said — foreign hostility?

No! We are in our own country and we wish our country peace and quiet. It is here we want our daily bread. We do not look to left or right, to East or West! But whatever the country's labour has produced should be destined to the working people of Poland, because "a worker justly deserves his reward" (I, Tim 5, 18). What a man's work has made, he has first rights to.

We wish it to be just so in our country. If we were to look only to what we might import from elsewhere, we should live perpetually in want. We ought to produce all this ourselves. But to achieve this we need to act in the right spirit — in the spirit of the Gospel. ... there is no need to search out enemies here or anywhere else. We should rather mobilize our forces to work. We should turn to wisdom, to common-sense, we should respect man, his rights and his work by guaranteeing him social freedom. Then we can have everything in our country without help from anybody, without foreign borrowing which costs us so much...

... Alas, it is otherwise now in Poland: we have to save the world at the cost of Poland. This disturbs the social order, which must be repaired post haste, if our country is to remain peaceful and in harmonious co-existence and co-operation, and if the country is to achieve economic order.

152

It is a disaster to be preoccupied with the whole world at the expense of one's own country. We, Poles, need institutions of one sort or another to keep law and order but here in Poland, not in the wide world. When we shall have achieved just that, when our children shall have been cared for adequately fed and educated — and I do not speak even of welfare but only of necessities — then the Polish nation will not deny help to others in need. But this order may not be disturbed and one may not save the world forgetful of one's own country and one's duties to one's nation.

..The Gospel has the power — without any grandiose plans — to bring order to our social, moral, professional, economic and political life. There is no reason to fear the Gospel, indeed Christ came not to kill but to save. And we are not here to hinder anyone, but to help, serve and support. That is our position. That is why we were so sensitive in those difficult moments to the plight of our workers, be it in Ursus or in Radom. Because that too is among our duties — to take compassion on our brothers and to help them when they are not able to help themselves.

I often repeat that there is no reason to fear either the Church, or the Bishops or the clergy of Poland, because by the will of the Creator they are allies of divine order and in consequence of economic order. We are not economists, we have no ambition of entering those spheres of competence, to abrogate lay authority. We are here that the evangelic spirit may permeate everything and that we may help in this very spirit.."

Distrust and enforced propagation of atheism

On 26 August '76 Primate preached to 15,000 pilgrims who had gathered at Częstochowa on the feast of Our Lady of Częstochowa for ceremonies preparatory to the 600th anniversary (which is to take place in 1982) of the Miraculous Picture of the Blessed Virgin. He made known that the Bishops had in a letter appealed to the Government to put an end to the arrests, the police interrogations and inquiries and to show instead magnanimity. He also took up the issue of confidence in the government and argued that the propagation of atheism officially introduced into the school curricula was, as a form of constraint, a further cause of distrust among the population:

"... for the sake of social and economic redevelopment and its effectiveness, in order that the life of our country be prosperous and peaceful we should set aside anything that might endanger distrust towards the implementation of the development programme.

We well know the breadth of the industrial development programme. But how it lacks success. Exactly so, there is distrust. It stems from the fact that those who mean our country ill — I know not why nor at whose behest — have inflicted on Poland the propagation of political atheism, and this has harmful repercussions on our much needed economic and social development.

... If we expect greater effectiveness in our efforts, so necessary in the field of economic development, let us take steps to free ourselves of this imposed political atheization."

As to reprisals against workers, he saw them as serving no other purpose than to "undermine the authority and dignity of government" and was quick to suggest that the number of prisons be halved and their warders more usefully employed in those sectors of industry where the supply of labour was insufficient.

Documents prepared by the 154th Plenary Conference of the Episcopate

The official propagation of atheism was discussed at large at the 154th Plenary Conference of the Episcopate (8–10 September). The Plenary Conferences are held about six times a year and discuss current problems facing the Church in Poland. We have mentioned how Kąkol's briefing on the Party's attitude to religion had been leaked to the Western press (earlier section). In an effort to mollify the impression Kąkol had caused, Gierek had implied in a speech to workers at Mielec (3 September) that there was harmony between State and Church. The Conference decidedly put the record straight in a number of documents.

First, in the Conference Communiqué where the issue of confidence is also touched:

"§2 ... Conference, having discussed moral and social problems which have lately arisen in Poland, approved the letter addressed in July by the Primate and Secretary of the Episcopate to the Government. The letter dealt with some disturbing incidents which took place at the end of June. The country is in need of stability and order more than ever. Conference is of the opinion that the authorities must show respect for the civil rights of the individual. The Government should conduct a genuine dialogue with the people and take notice of their wishes when making decisions affecting the whole community. Conference requests the authorities to cease reprisals against workers who took part in protest action

154

against the unnecessarily high increases in food prices planned by the Government for June 1976. The workers concerned should be reinstated in their employment and their social and legal status restored. A compensation should be paid to those who have suffered and an amnesty should be declared.

Considering that the economic situation of the country is at present difficult, all citizens are under an obligation to bring about improvement. Conference, accordingly, appeals to all sections of the community to intensify their efforts, show greater workmanship, be prepared to practise self-denial for the common good and to keep the peace. Good workmanship is a moral duty and the capacity for self denial a Christian virtue. However, the conditions for good workmanship and self-denial are always: confidence in the authorities, and that can only be achieved if the authorities show real concern and care for the welfare of all citizens. Only by common efforts may we overcome the difficulties which our country faces."

The document goes on to record the current anxieties of the Episcopate: first, with regard to directives issued at the beginning of the new school year by the education authorities (these encouraged the introduction of lay rituals designed to oust corresponding religious ceremony), secondly, with regard to the distressing increase in numbers of divorces. Church documents show much concern for the family as the basic social unit (see also p. 161).

Discrimination against believers

The same Conference documented its grievances in a closely reasoned Episcopal Letter (read out in all churches on 28 November). After a moving preamble stressing the importance of faith to one's self-motivation and self-reconciliation, the letter reads:

"... [the State] has no right to act maliciously towards religion and against the citizen's freedom of conscience and of religious observance. Such conduct is an infringement first and foremost of the natural rights of a citizen. It is this natural law which provides foundation for the resolutions of any constitution or international declaration such as, for example, the U.N. Charter of Human Rights, which guarantees every citizen the freedom of religion and observance. In our country the great majority of citizens are believers and are members of the Catholic Church. If then state officials make war on religion they are guilty of abuse towards the citizens whose taxes pay for their services. The fight against religion is paid for with funds to which the practising Catholic must contribute. Who can fail to see the extraordinary contradiction behind this sad state of affairs."

` The letter complains how building regulations are used to check the progress of religion; how building permission for new churches, especially in new towns, is delayed interminably (an earlier conference communiqué of April puts the desired number of churches at a modest 500); how practising catholics are discriminated against by being barred from senior appointments and by not gaining deserved promotions. The letter condemns the method used in combatting religion: the open propagation of atheism in theatres, cinemas and television productions, the misrepresentation of Scripture, the ridiculing of religious observance, the increase of pornographic literature and shows. Much attention focuses on the ways in which the State seeks to estrange youth from religion. In the schools and universities the young are told that a religious outlook is in direct contradiction to the discoveries of modern science. At holiday camps the young are prevented from going to Mass and are not even permitted to wear medallions or crosses. Students are subjected to threats, reprisals, long questioning to deter them from using the facilities of the academic chaplaincy. The letter pointed out that "one leading state dignitary had disclosed that new dates for school holidays were to be proposed so that they would no longer coincide with the liturgical calender."

Conference also prepared a document read in the church on 19 September (Communications Sunday). This was widely reported in the West.

"... We cannot remain silent when basic civil rights and among them the right to religious freedom are not fully respected. We cannot remain silent when the Church is refused the right to have and freely use the media of social communication which are so indispensable today to the carrying out of the mission which God has entrusted to her. The Church has been denied access to many of the media and hence her power of moral influence has been severely limited.

We cannot remain silent when a section of the press propagates sexual laxity, demoralizes children and youth. Neither can we remain silent when harmful magazines and books which undermine the principles of Christianity, are published in editions running into several thousands; yet permission is not granted for the publication of [religious] text-books, and other catechetic aids nor even of First-Communion Prayer Books."

In his sermon the following Sunday (26 September) the Primate once more considered the issue of Church–State relations. Referring to Gierek's speech at Mielec he had this to say:

"We have recently heard statements to the effect that there is no longer any controversy between State and Church. But controversies do exist and they have been listed in a communiqué issued by the Bishops' Conference at Jasnogóra [in Częstochowa]."

He reminded the congregation that the Episcopate had appealed to the government on behalf of the workers and continued that: "it was painful when workers must struggle for their rights from a workers' government. In such a situation Polish Bishops have to remember their duties to the working people." This last sentence is taken to imply support for the Workers' Defence Committee which had just come into existence. The sermon then considered two other social questions: first the disquieting recent statistics that 60% of Warsaw families had only one child and, secondly, that labour was being sent abroad when it was in short supply at home (reference to 4,500 workers who had just been sent to East Germany to build a colliery).

Austerity but only at the price of freedom

On Saturday 6 November the Cardinal preached in Ostrów (Great Poland region) when a copy of the Miraculous Picture of Our Blessed Lady of Częstochowa was to journey through the archdiocese of Poznań. He once more returned to current problems stressing in particular the crucial importance of freedom in all aspects of everyday life:

"As we work and toil, as we embark on all manner of labour, let us not forget one thing, that in carrying out the duties of the day, of the occupation, in goodly fashion, we still desire and demand that our land be a land of Christ, a land of Mary. We are ready for many a drudgery, effort, privation and even sacrifice but only at the price of breathing the spirit of freedom in our home.

It is this spirit of freedom that the Nation is fighting for today — workers, intelligentsia, the bishops and priests. If our prayers be at any time pertinent then surely it is when we sing our hymn "Lord bless our country free". Be there no reservation, no let up in our prayer! ... Let it be free internally, free in its own country, free in confessing its faith, free in acknowledging God in any office, in every walk of life. Free in the home, free in the school, in the workshop, in the office, in government agencies, in the army, everywhere — be it ours, native, Polish and free. Where there is a will, the more so shall our prayers be heart-felt, sincere, the more so shall we be mobilized to any toil or struggle.

We wish to live in peace — but not be dormant. We wish to live under conditions which will allow us to feel that, after having gone through thick and thin, having traversed the sea of blood let by Poles at front lines and in concentration camps, we have a right to live and work in our country in the spirit of freedom. No declaration and no speeches can be a substitute for its motive force, which may solely be guaranteed by the realities of everyday life.

We stand here, the Children of God, between a church and a prison. Here it was in the region of Great Poland in this very prison that Cardinal Primate Ledóchowski[1] was held for two years. For what reason? Because he stood up to defend the freedom of the faith. He defended the freedom of the Nation and of the Church. He found himself imprisoned for having defended freedom. And whilst it was prison that held the man who fought for freedom, it is a church that offers man freedom — freedom of spirit, of heart, of mind.

We wish our country to have as few prisons as possible and as many churches as possible. It is in the churches that freedom of the Nation is tendered and safe-kept: prisons should be the exception and not the rule for government.

When Polish workers on the streets of Radom and Ursus cried out for their right to subsistence they were rarely appreciated. Already in July, we personally wrote to the principal state and party authorities with the request: set these people free; everyone has the right to expression — within the limits of a normal declaration of demand. They are not guilty, though at times the demonstrations took on improper proportions. The multitude of workers anxious for the livelihood of their families, had every right to expression. It is for this reason that they should not be punished by prisons, courts police interrogation and other harassments of which we are well aware. We therefore asked the State authorities: bring an end to it, this is no way to win favour with the Nation, which wishes to be free not only in work but in the expression of its convictions."

---

1) **Mieczysław Ledóchowski** (1822–1902) was Archbishop of Gniezno and Poznań, from 1874 to 1876; was imprisoned by the Prussian government for opposing Bismarck's *Kulturkampf;* ordained Cardinal, sentenced to exile, he became Prefect of the Congregation for the Propagation of the Faith, in Rome.

Support for fund raising on behalf of workers

In a sermon on Sunday 5 December the Primate sought inspiration from the example of St. Francis of Assisi whose 750th anniversary was being celebrated. Drawing upon the Saint's special relationship to Man and Nature, the Primate preached a brotherly love extending to a deep respect for the environment. He contrasted this against the prevailing view of nature as raw material for production and with the kind of treatment that the workers of Ursus had suffered. The Cardinal disclosed that he knew details of 33 workers who had been arrested and of whom all but four had been beaten and sent on the infamous "health trot". The Primate's lesson on the joys to be reaped from adopting a programme of Christian love and aloofness from "the fashionable ideals of a consumption economy" brought a message of implied support for the fund raising activities of the Workers' Defence Commitee:

"Certainly we cannot imitate St. Francis in everything, but Man must stand above the whole material order. He must preserve a measure of independence in relation to the dire conditions in which he finds himself at times. Let us remember that there are those who are poorer and hungrier than we, particularly families deprived of husbands and fathers — who are confined to prison. I have in my possession a long list of just such women, who have been left by themselves with small children and mothers who are sick and lonely. Let us be mindful of them. They need to be noticed and we should hasten to help them and should ourselves learn to do without, especially to do without luxuries and commodities beyond the standards of our social environment, in order that we may bring help. That would be in the spirit of [franciscan] poverty, that would be a transformation of matter into the spirit of Christian love."

Just wages and basic rights of work

On Sunday 12 December the Cardinal took up the issue of a just wage and the role of trade unions. In addressing himself to such an area he took the view expressed earlier that:

"When in 1848 Emanuel Kettler, Bishop of Mainz, wrote his "Die Arbeiterfrage" and in that same year Marx published his *Communist Manifesto* the workers' lot was more or less the same as today. You might say: but that is simplistic reasoning. Yet, it is supported by experiences and observations which it is hard to speak of now. The working world had then to fight for its right of subsistence and for its social rights. Often it had to stand up against the governing political system."

On the subject of wages, the Cardinal was of the opinion that workers who do not receive a just reward for their work should demand wage increases. Earnings should be such as would adequately keep them and their families. He insisted that the trade unions should not have political aims. Their raison d'être is to demand just wages and humane conditions. If social justice had reigned in Poland the uprisings in 1956, in 1970 and recently in summer would not have taken place. Ill-paid workers were forced to protest against excessive food prices. He urged workers not to seek employment in several jobs simultaneously as is frequently practised. They should keep to one job and do it well and demand a just wage — one which would suffice for their families' needs.

On 14 April he quoted a specific example of severe working conditions and the implications this held for government. The topic was also discussed by the 158th Episcopal Conference (4–5 May 1977):

"I have read today the letter from the Bishops of Katowice — from the Bishop Ordinary and his auxiliaries — to the [party] authorities. This letters uncovers the overwhelming tragedy of exhaustion suffered by our miners, who under pressure from propaganda machinery have hardly one free Sunday in a month, as not until after three consecutive Sundays have been used for mining, might the fourth turn out to be free. But should there be a "free Saturday",[2] the miner has to go down the pit on the Sunday which was to have been free. The letter cites a number of instances which are the result of this: people dying of heart attack in their youth. Perhaps at times they are incorrectly motivated to earn quickly, as one young man who wished to build himself a home and accepted work right, left and centre. But he did not get to live in it — only his coffin was borne out of it. He used his strength up prematurely.

One can be a pace-setter at work but a state of affairs cannot be allowed where a man, who cannot himself understand how important it is to take rest after heavy work, is encouraged to further superhuman effort. He should indeed be induced to rest, lest he should think that silver and gold is everything..."

---

2) In 1976 only one Saturday in four was a day off from work.

Memorandum on Population Policies

On 21 January 1977 the Episcopate sent a document outlining their views on population growth to the Government. Below are extracts from a summary published by the Episcopate on 21 March.

"... The number of children barely equals the numerical size of their parents' generation. One more step in this direction and as a Nation we shall cease to reproduce, and when at some moment there are fewer children than parents, soon ˙ after the population of the country must fall.

Admittedly there has been a certain improvement in these last years. Post-war cohorts are reaching marriageable age and the average number of children in a family has risen slightly (to about 2.2) in consequence of a rise in living standards and of the changing climate surrounding family affairs. Nevertheless danger levels are still imminent. Material circumstances, particularly with regard to accommodation of young families, remain difficult and threaten to grow worse... Of particular importance are differences between town and country and between rich and poor. For 15 years we have been reproducing as a nation thanks to the peasant population where the average family has 3 children, whilst the average town family is not completely reproducing since it has between 1.7 and 1.8 children. However, the peasant population is increasingly becoming a minority, is ageing quickly and changing over to an urban way of life. In the major cities the average is one child per family and the only-child is predominant in both nursery-schools and the schools.

What is worse, we reproduce on the whole through poor ˙ families, those less well fed, less well clothed and less well off in health. Those socially better-off — intelligentsia, technical staff, and highly skilled workers — usually have one child, rarely two, and one third of married couples in this group have no children at all.

... The country's progress requires establishment of an optimal rythm of generation replacement and of population growth. The working population should rear a sufficiently large young population to take its place but a working generation needs to be sufficiently large in order not to be excessively burdened with the upkeep of the older generation. This requires a moderately expanded reproduction of the population. ... A moderately expanded generation replacement would require an average of about 2.5 children per family to

be achieved and maintained over a longer period. This requires a definite increase in the number of families with 3 or
more children. There should be at least 50% of these ...
Social policies pursued by government should remove the
obstacles hindering the development of the family and of the
nation and investments in population policies should grow at
least as quickly as the national income ... Only ⅓ of newly-
weds have their own home. There is a dearth of acccomoda-
tion to the extent of 1 million homes and the deficit is rising.
Waiting-time in the housing co-operatives runs to over a dozen
years ... Lack of accomodation means that postponed child-
bearing leads to no child-bearing at all.

We therefore need to increase investment in the accommodation sector, expand the co-operatives and particularly increase the provision of building materials and credits for
building in rural areas, also we need to give priority to
families with many children and to young couples. Young
couples should be given long-term loans to obtain and furnish
a home and such loans should be partly remitted as and when
children are born.

... According to many sociologists and social politicians,
employment of mothers is too high in Poland. At the same
time chronic supply difficulties and high prices of children's
articles form an extra burden for the over-worked mother.

... A system of part-time employment should be instituted,
home industry encouraged, convenient hours and employment
near the home assured. ... Women leaving work because of
children should gain some financial compensation and a
guarantee of return to work and of professional retraining.

A third problem is that of compensating to a level of
minimum social necessity the income of families with many
children, of families where the mother is not at work, and
of single parent families. Family benefits still form a very
small percentage of the total income and pay from 5 to 15%
of the expense of child rearing. ... To help mothers who do
not earn income, a tutelage allowance should be created and
be paid over a period of between 1 to 3 years to mothers
bearing or rearing a child."

*The document goes on to point out the role of the mass-media in
this programme. Hitherto they have been projecting an image associating progress with limitation on number of children. Also reviewed is
the question of abortion and its part in lowering population growth*

(the annual number of abortions is officially estimated at a quarter of a million and put at half a million by some unofficial sources).

Vows of Jasnogóra: 3 May 1977

' *The focal point for the Church's work in the first half of 1977 was the renewal of Vows made originally on 26th August 1956 at Jasnogóra (Częstochowa) — two months after the Poznań uprising. They were renewed in 1977 on May 3rd, feast of the Blessed Virgin, Queen of Poland, a significant date in the history of Poland and a national though unofficial feast. On May 3rd 1791, the Polish Sejm (Parliament) crowned four years of debate over political reform by passing the "Constitution of May the 3rd", a constitution laying the foundations of a more modern state administration and abolishing various, albeit not all, privileges which had hampered the Nation's progress.*

The Vows of Jasnogóra gave expression to the Church's social programme: loyalty to God; defence of human life (including life of the unborn); defence of the inviolability of marriage and of the family; justice (just treatment of workers, non-discrimination against believers); determination to fight such national defects as alcoholism; the honouring of the Blessed Virgin as Queen of Poland. Their current relevance was emphasized by the Polish Hierarchy in a Pastoral Letter (read out in the churches on 24th April). Renewal of the vows once more brought to public attention the pressing problems of the Church, the substance of which has been stated in the earlier documents reviewed above.

At the renewal ceremony the Primate pointed out the deep tradition in which the vows were rooted:

"Each of us is in conscience bound to be vigilant, lest there be killing with impunity, lest there be loss of life. This obligation rests on everyone: mothers-to-be, judiciary, police, political or party authorities.

The Nation has a duty to watch over its greatest treasure which is Man — the citizen. The State exists to ensure for its citizens the necessary conditions for subsistence and for life in freedom to within the limits of the fundamental human rights which he fulfils. If as once [in 1656] the King stood up for the underprivileged and in his Vows of Lwów declared the enfranchisement of the farming population, if later the Constitution of May the 3rd [1791] was also to take up the cause of the underprivileged, then too the Vows of Jasnogóra of 20 years ago take their place in this tradition. Today we are, moreover, supported in our Christian demands by such international documents as the "Charter of Human and Civil Rights"."

What merits notice is that the Primate used much sterner language in this address:

"We have already said that rights must correspond to duties. Each Christian has in his native land not only obligations but also rights. That is why it is time to speak in Poland of the rights of believers. Though we have been speaking of them for a long time, we have been using delicate language: we have been requesting that the religious rights of a baptised nation be respected. There are times however when it is not enough to request. Possessing rights we have also the duty to demand that in our country the believer should be protected by the law."

Chapter seven

PERSPECTIVES FOR THE FUTURE

PROGRAMME OF THE POLISH
LEAGUE FOR INDEPENDENCE

A natural sequel and enlargement upon the postulates expressed in the Manifesto of the 59 appeared in the early months of 1976 in a samizdat document entitled "The Programme of the Polish League for Independence". It formulates a comprehensive range of long-term aims for the whole nation and justifies itself on the grounds that:

"Many events indicate that there is a growing need in our country for a programme which would not only express the public discontentment but would also contain definite postulates and long-term aims... Our society consists of disconnected groupings and circles whose mutual intercourse and co-operation the Party strives to vitiate. We wish the programme by its very existence to focus our thinking and to allow a co-ordination of the actions of all those who, though lacking organizational unity, shall be united by a vision of our common goal."

The PLI have issued a number of discussion documents which lack of space does not permit to cite here. The main points of the programme, and their reasoned justification, may be gleaned from a reading of the following abridgement.

Countries subordinate to Moscow, that is the so-called "socialist bloc" and the USSR itself, are in a state of permanent although concealed crisis. The latter is caused by growing internal tensions, the discontent of oppressed nations, the malfunctioning economy of the whole system and the failure to keep up with those countries that favour unrestricted technilogical, social, and cultural development. ...

It is impossible to foresee the moment when the crisis will erupt in all its severity. ... We must make every conceivable effort to act in concert and not leave the task of struggling for violated rights of the whole nation to a single social group.

Our program is based on the following principles:

1. The nation... is sovereign and thus has the inalienable right to freely decide its own destiny.

2. All citizens are, without exception, equal before the law and should be given the same opportunity to lead their own lives.

3. The overwhelming majority of Poles profess religious beliefs, and most are Catholics. The prevailing political system in Poland cannot be based on discrimination against that majority.

4. The Polish state and nation have traditionally been distinguished by a continuous expansion in the realm of civil liberties, while new social groups have constantly been drawn into the government of the country and given joint responsibility for its fate. From the 16th century on, Polish political thought has made outstanding contributions to democratic ideas and the concept of liberty. The system of totalitarian autocracy imposed upon us is not only foreign to our national traditions, but also anachronistic and humiliating.

Their 26 point programme was as follows:

1. ...We consider all post-war agreements... limiting the sovereignty of the Republic, to have been made under duress without consulting the will of the people and therefore to be invalid. The right to assume obligations which would be legally and morally binding on all Poles, can only be exercised by a freely-elected Polish Parliament whose activities are not subject to foreign pressure.

2. The confidence of society in the apparatus of state government has virtually been destroyed by the experience of the last 30 years. This has resulted in widespread cynicism and the threat of anarchy, which is dangerous for the nation as it is for every government.... The post-war system of government is based on lies and secrecy of action. ...The principles of openness and confidence should be re-introduced into social and political life. Citizens have a right to know the truth about all matters in which they are involved.

3. Legal and economic discrimination... of social groups, (peasantry, skilled workers, religious orders, all believers, etc.), combined with the artificial... elevation of, and showering of privileges upon party members and other adherents of the régime, are distinctly harmful and lead to a substantial impoverishment of the nation's human resources. ...Total equality of rights of all citizens regardless of their descent, denomination,

166

organizational affiliation is a fundamental requirement to remedy the present situation ...

4. We are drowning in lies, "Sovereignty" signifies obedience to the USSR, "security" means the ubiquitous secret police, while "freedom" is the absence of choice. It is necessary to cleanse public life of layers of deceit which humiliate, stupefy and choke us ... The words Country, independence, democracy, freedom, socialism, equality and justice must be given their due meaning and respect.

5. ... All citizens should persistently demand adherence to the rule of law.

6. ... Freely elected representatives of the people, as well as individuals, should have the right and the means to verify whether obligations are honoured and justice administered.

7. ... The healthy development of the nation is prevented by the absence of a free exchange of ideas. ... Freedom of speech is not just a luxury for intellectuals but a basic need for everyone. Reinstatement of the freedom of speech is one of our fundamental tasks.

8. ... The postulates of confidence between the public and the authorities, of total equality, and of public control cannot be realized without the freedom of association. ...

9. ... Education of children and youth in the Polish People's Republic is increasingly aimed not so much at cultivating the minds and characters but at bringing up obedient citizens ... We demand that schools be free of deceit, terror and political and police pressures.

10. ... The Polish universities must regain their autonomy. Elections to the academic courts of government should be carried out without any political or police pressures.

11. ... The Catholic Church, whose enormous moral authority was consolidated by resistance to German occupation and communist persecution, should regain full freedom of action and be enabled to fulfill all its functions. ...

12. ... Our political significance is being squandered and compromised by our slavish role of an obedient satellite of the USSR. ... Polish foreign policy should be pursued in accordance with our current interests and with our traditions of liberty. Only then may we rebuild our international stature as an independent state ...

13. The most vital factor governing Polish foreign policy is that of relations with Russia ... A blanket of silence is thrown

over the unprovoked attack on Poland in 1939 by the Soviet Union allied to Fascist Germany, the later deportations of millions of Polish citizens, their frightful sufferings, the death of many thousands, the murder in the Eastern territories of the greater part of Poland's intelligentsia, and the crime of Katyń. ... A genuine friendship between Poland and Russia could be achieved in the future but only if mutual relations are based on sincerity, on an open acknowledgement of the wrongs inflicted on Poland and on *de facto* genuine sovereign equality of rights.

14. Russia is not our neighbour. Our neighbours to the East are the Ukraine, Byelorussia and Lithuania... The Ukrainian, Byelorussian, Lithuanian, Estonian and Latvian nations are not independent today... and are subjected to a more severe political, ideological and religious discipline than Poland. We make no territorial claims on our eastern neighbours, though the loss of Lvov and Vilnius, despite their centuries-long links with Polish culture, is and will remain very painful. We demand, however, ... that Poles living there should be guaranteed equal rights and allowed to preserve their language and national culture. We also demand that Poles from Poland should have unhindered access to those places which are connected with the history of our nation and our former common state.

15. Polish-German relations, overshadowed by the enormity of German crimes against Poland during the last war, are further complicated by another factor... Many facts tending to illustrate the spontaneous development within the German Federal Republic of views and feelings conductive to a far-reaching understanding between the two nations, are never allowed to become public knowledge. Complete bilateral exchange of information, free exchange of thought and of people constitute the only possible method of closing our long-protracted disputes.

16. The European [Economic] Community, though ignored and ridiculed by communist propaganda, despite various difficulties is developing so well that it continues to attract new members... and new advocates (for example, the Italian Communist Party). This group of nations which, in view of its economic characteristics, is our most important trade partner, is also our most natural ideological ally. ... The closest possible links with the Community will be our best guarantee against the resurgence of conflicts with Germany.

168

17. ... The free collaboration between Polish organizations and communities at home and abroad is prevented. The Polish emigration is a priceless national fund of opportunities and experience ... and their familiarity with the functioning of contemporary democratic states might help us to eliminate the consequences of many years of totalitarian government in Poland.

18. ... Every Pole, not facing court proceedings, should be issued a passport on demand and allowed to keep it.

19. ... An independent and constructive re-assessment of both the economic possibilities of our country and its place in the European and world economies, is necessary. Also needed is an elaboration of new principles for the social division of labour.

20. The Party, deprived of moral authority [and backing] ... seeks to curry the favour of at least some sections of society ... Let us neither relinquish our freedom of opinion and activity for short-lived privileges, nor barter our dignity and conscience for bonuses and motor cars. If we do not sell ourselves — the authorities will be forced to make concessions and to enlarge our scope of freedom.

21. ... The maintenance of the Ministry of the Interior alone costs us more than the Polish state spends on education, health care, and cultural matters combined. At the same time, the housing situation constantly deteriorates and the official waiting period for accommodation will soon reach 8 to 10 years. The sick are left lying for weeks in hospital corridors. If the above mentioned sums ... were turned over to the needs of the housing industry, each year would bring a million homes and a few thousand hospital beds.

22. ... At all levels the Polish economy is subordinated to political aims, needs, and whims. The fact that the same people run the politico-governmental apparatus and the administrative machinery of the economy is unhealthy ... ministries and other official bodies rivalize for investment credits and raw materials on the basis not of needs but of Party influence ... Politics and economics should be consistently separated.

23. ... It is of absolute importance to involve the workers of all state-owned businesses in their co-management ... For this the worker councils must become independent and have the right to oppose decisions from on high. Workers should directly and openly share in the profits, they should be al-

lowed to become share-holders of the firms where they work.
24. ... The government should maintain its control of the
key industries and in particular of the energy sector. However, advantage should be taken of existing private capital to
form large-scale share-holdings ... housing and consumer goods
industries would then develop faster and more comprehen-
sively.
25. ... The potential of Polish agriculture is pitifully under-
exploited ... an outrage in view of the permanent scarcity of
food on the home market. Farmers must be guaranteed owner-
ship of the land which they till, thus removing the spectre of
collectivization.
26. Marketing and services are an area of the economy which
makes everyday life a misery particularly for women. ... Here
the state monopoly is at its most senseless. Thousands of shops
... run at a loss instead of profit. The state-run businesses and
co-operatives should limit themselves to large-scale operations
such as transportation, ware-houses and supermarkets. All the
remaining networks of shops and services would operate more
efficiently and profitably if left in private hands and to small,
spontaneously formed, joint-stock companies.

... It is therefore the pressing duty of all who refuse to
sanction the present situation and who disagree with Party
policies, to take an active stand.

... This is primarily a task for the active Polish intelligentsia ... and of the largest social group, the industrial
workers who possess the greatest power. The exprience of the
last 30 years has shown that power to be invincible.

The Polish League for Independence

INTERVIEW WITH KUROŃ

*The following is a translation of M. Lucbert's interview with Kuroń
(Le Monde, 29 January 1977) and should be read in conjunction with
Kuroń's explanatory remarks summarized on p. 175.*

— In the last few weeks we have witnessed several trials
of workers arrested during or after the events of June 1976.
You have just come back from Radom where a man has been
tried — six and a half months after the alleged events were
committed — on a charge of participating in the ransacking
of the party headquarters of this town. What happened at the
trial?

— The trial I have attended passed without disturbance. Politically the new and interesting fact is that there were many policemen in the precincts and even in the corridors of the court-house. Workers had come to protect members of the Committee, but we advised them to withdraw. Apparently after the incidents at the beginning of the month the central authorities wanted to show that they did not wish a repetition of any similar provocation and they took matters in hand. In my opinion, the provocations were aimed not so much against members of the Committee as against the tribunal, against the judiciary. Party officials at local level are far greater hard-liners than those at central level. They are afraid lest the leadership should waver in the face of a wave of protest. On the other hand, however, the government cannot afford not to take due account of the indignation expressed by the president of the tribunal who stated that, under such conditions, justice could not be administered.

IT IS WE WHO TOLERATE THE GOVERNMENT

— The Workers' Defence Committee has been declared illegal by the authorities, and yet it continues to exist. How do you explain this tolerance?

— The statement of the problem needs to be inverted: it is we who tolerate the government. That makes you smile? Let me give you an example. In Zielona Góra, at the Zastal foundry, the authorities wanted workers to sign a letter demanding that an end be put to the activities of the Committee, since it acts "counter to our sentiments and the norms prevailing in our country". Of the five thousand workers only one hundred and fifty-seven signed the text. If you discount members of the Party machine that does not leave many. In actual fact, this campaign for signatures, staged by the authorities, has turned out to be a demonstration in favour of the Committee. At the present moment, the authorities will have collected a total of seventeen thousand signatures against us, but had there even been a million, it would still have been a demonstration in our favour.

— You yourself and some other members of the Committee have recently been summoned by the police. Why?

— We have been interrogated as witnesses in an inquiry against X ... for spreading false information. A dossier is

171

being prepared which will be used to accuse us for having disseminated false information abroad about Poland. Several of us have been summoned before an administrative tribunal for "illegal collection of funds". This is only the beginning. The reprisals can only become more severe.

— Why would the authorities be committing such errors when they can hope that as soon as the trials are over, your action will have lost its *raison d'être?*

— I would dearly like to be mistaken. May I remind you, however, that our action will have no reason to cease when the trials are over. Our Committee has made its aims known: it demands amnesty for all who were convicted in connection with the June events; the creation of a Commission of Inquiry and detailed information on the extent of reprisals; punishment of the perpetrators of the violence and maltreatment, and, reinstatement of contract-workers with the preservation of all their previous rights.

— What in your view is the way out of the present crisis?

— It is not for me to advise the Party. But from their point of view, it seems to me they should institute structural reforms along the lines considered some time ago by Mr. Rakowski, managing editor of the weekly *Polityka.* They should seek to create institutional forms of consultation with society, attempt to engage in a dialogue. That is the necessary minimum.

Let us take the two most important problems of the day: prices and the critical food shortage.

Without a price reform it will be more and more difficult to heal the economy. But any decisions on this matter should be consented to by the workers. The authorities should, in their own interest, favour free election of delegates to autonomous representations, without these having necessarily to be capped by a nation-wide organization. I repeat that I am trying to bear in mind the point of view of the authorities. As for myself, I would go much further. I am in favour of independent trade unions.

The second problem is that of food supply. Its inadequacy is the result of policies aimed at destroying smallholdings. The agricultural population needs to be reassured. The peasants are uncertain of the future and have insufficient financial means. They put up passive resistance by refusing to sign delivery contracts with the State. But it is difficult under the circumstances to know how much stems from political opposition and how much from protection of economic interests. Especially, since the authorities are not always tactful: for example, before Christmas, the police set up control points on trunk roads to confiscate illegally slaughtered meat. Such methods painfully remind the peasants of the times of the war.

If the authorities had the courage to engage a policy of reform by small steps, they would to a certain extent, be able to check their problems. But to me that eventuality seems very unlikely. That, in my view is why, with the path to the democratization closed to them, they will have to choose the path of reprisal.

THE BITTER LESSON OF 1970

— During the upheavals of December 1970 on the Baltic Coast the working class showed a greater degree of organization than during the recent troubles in Radom or Ursus. How do you explain his phenomenon?

— The Polish Workers learned a bitter lesson during the events of 1970. When in January 1971 Mr. Gierek, the First Secretary, went up to Szczecin, he asked the shipyard strike committee not to demand a withdrawal of the price increases, justifying them on the grounds that they were indispensable to the Polish economy. The workers accepted his arguments. In exchange Mr. Gierek promised reforms in Union representation along with free election of delegates.

A month later it was the turn of the workers of the textile industry in Łódź to strike: the government backed out and rescinded the price increases. But at the same time the promised union reforms were never carried out. It should be said that Mr. Gierek undertook the trip to Szczecin against the majority advice of the political bureau. The workers drew from this the lesson that, even if they were allowed to elect freely a committee [of representation] it would be smothered with no end of promises. On 25th June last, Mr. Szydlak, an important member of the political bureau, went to a factory out on strike in Łódź. He asked to speak with a representation chosen by workers. This proposal brought a burst of laughter in reply.

— You have recently made public a political programme. Are you solely responsible, or are you spokesman for a group? — I assume sole responsibility. It is not strictly speaking a programme but, as the title indicates "reflections on a programme of action". I have confined myself to a polemic with certain groupings who themselves claim to have elaborated a programme. It is impossible to formulate programmes under the present conditions. More modestly I propose ideas for debate which would serve to prepare the groundwork for such a programme.

A SORT OF FINLANDIZATION

— What political label could one tie to your reflections? — None. The political classifications current in the West are not valid here. My text is addressed to the Poles, not to the government. It does not demand reforms and urges only the necessity of a policy of short steps as I explained a moment ago.

The present rulers have created a type of apparatchik that does not know how to hold discussions with the people. When problems arise, he goes into hiding. Mr. Gierek himself does know how to make contact, but he is the last, or almost the last, to do so. With one or two exceptions none of today's rulers know how to talk to a strike committee. Believe you me, I am well placed to know it. I was brought up an apparatchik.

Today the whole party machine knows that matters are taking a turn for the worse and they resist. They find Gierek too liberal and refuse to enter on the path of reform. In my reflections I try to explain how to create movements which would oblige the authorities to carry out reforms. That could, for example, be one of the functions of the Defence Committee which could play a role analogous to that played by worker councils in Spain. That is why I am proposing as watchword a "Third Poland of social movements".

— You have also shown yourself to be in favour of a sort of "Finlandization" of Poland. What exactly do you mean by that?

— The point of departure is this idea of a "Third Poland of social movements". Our country's representatives should come to a direct understanding with the USSR regarding the limits of reform. There is no need to be blinded by the Czechoslovak experience into believing these limits to be fixed once and for all. If within the leadership there are no forces capable of entering into this dialogue, then social movements, though marginal at present, could foster this evolution by reason of their influence and of pressure on the present hierarchy. In any case various indications lead me to believe that certain people or certain groupings within the party could come into the play of opposition forces. This way it would no longer be the party on its own but Polish society in almost all its entirety who could bargain from the Russians a status similar to that of Finland. It remains a question whether the authorities are not already too compromised to make it worth staking on this tactic. And one must not count on the Church, because, as the only genuine authority that there is today in Poland, it has become a fundamental adversary of the system.

A DISCLAIMER TO THE INTERVIEW

In a letter to "Le Monde" J. Kuroń points out that the above text is not a correct rendering of his views. He explains that:

1. Having said that "authentic worker representations (at least at management level) are indispensable to the proper running of the country", the WDC cannot play a role analogous to that of the Spanish worker councils, because the WDC is not and cannot be a workers' representation.

2. The Church is not and cannot be the source of political initiative, not because it is a "fundamental adversary of the system", but because the aims it serves cannot have a political character. Nonetheless the Church in "being the highest moral authority in the country, opposes totalitarianism".

3. The sense of social movements "encompasses all kind of action by individuals or small groups, which by virtue of their most general aims, form in combination a wide-scale action of importance to the whole community". In this meaning social movements have existed continually "at least since

175

1954, though the degree of integration and organization varied at different times". However, "their activity is radically constrained not just by, or even primarily by, the reprisals applied by government authorities. The fundamental factor which constrains the social action towards democratization is consciousness of Soviet military power. ... Poles may win sovereignty only in combined effort with other captive nations of the Soviet empire, ... but this programme cannot be realized today. Yet today a deep crisis is destroying the life of Polish society and cannot be overcome without the simultaneous overthrow of a system guarded by Soviet tanks. I am convinced that this quadrature of the circle can be resolved, that is, totalitarianism may be overcome without risk of a suicidal clash with the military power of the USSR." Social and economic crisis, dependence on the West and on Japan "permits the inference that the Soviet leadership fears armed intervention in Poland. But that does not imply that such intervention is impossible, rather it implies that Moscow would be prepared to make many concessions. ... the only strength of the PZPR [the Party] leadership in their dialogue with the eastern neighbour lies in social movements in Poland." Instead of basing themselves on this strength, the various leaderships contained them, until these turned against them. "... one cannot yet exclude that there are no forces within the PZPR able to understand this obvious truth and willing to draw conclusions." In the meantime Polish society should organize social movements; their "strategies and · tactics, including diplomacy, should be publicly formulated" and they should articulate their aims for the present and those aims for the future "which we have at present to surrender in the face of force". Such a movement should necessarily demand that Moscow formulate her conditions: "if you do not wish armed intervention, formulate your threat before you need to carry it out".

4. On the subject of political labels: "The opposition: totalitarianism as against pluralism, to me seems the essential criterion in modern times for differentiation of political action, of standpoint and of programmes. I do not wish to make the traditional division into political camps. That would obscure what is most important."

VIVE LA POLOGNE!

In recent years the Polish Government has had a good press in Western Europe. Journalists have praised the modernization of Poland's cities, drawn attention to economic expansion and pointed to a certain liberalization. Nevertheless, opposition to the policies of the Party leadership is manifest in all sections of society — the events of the last twelve months were proof of this. How can this be explained?

Let us recall the facts. From December 1975 to March 1976 the Poles were involved in a heated controversy on the issue of amendments to the Constitution. In this strange debate — whose only trace in the official press was a brief passage in a report of a speech by the President of the Council of State — writers, journalists, actors, musicians, professors and students made a stand against the amendments proposed by the Government. According to unofficial sources originating from the Party Central Committee, 40,000 citizens had submitted in writing criticism of the amendments, whose object was to guarantee a leading role for the Communist Party and to affirm the permanence of Poland's alliance with the USSR.

A month after this debate, there was a protest in academic circles against the expulsion of Jacek Smykał from the Medical Academy in Szczecin. This student had asked embarassing questions during a seminar in political science and had subsequently refused to sign a "declaration of loyalty" for the Security Service. There were precedents for this expulsion; but never had measures of this kind created such a stir of protest — for the first time since 1968 several hundred students signed an open letter of protest. Once again discontent among the intelligentsia seemed to foreshadow a general crisis.

The events of 25 June confirmed this diagnosis. In one day the Party leadership found itself facing the possibility of a general strike with the whole country on the brink of revolution. Why did the local Party secretary in Radom have to leave his office secretly to escape the wrath of workers, just as his counterpart in Szczecin was forced to do in 1970?

Mr. Gierek's team drew certain conclusions from Mr. Gomułka's tragic experience. They took into account the needs of the consumers. They seemed also to have realized that severe reprisals against opposition do not achieve their purpose. The new leadership also understood that to rescind a . decision once taken was a sign not of weakness but of good sense. This does not imply that there is a liberal or "Dubček-like revisionist" trend within the Party — rather, it indicates that those in power are now able to act in their own interests.

The emphasis placed on consumption has given rise to new desires. People are no longer content with being better off than they were six years before — they expect constant improvement in their standards. The revolt of June 1976 was ' not one of people who were starving, but of people who had had enough of being treated like sheep. It arose as a reaction not only to the increase in prices, but also to the manner of its justification by the propaganda machine. The people no longer trust the verbal assurances of those in power: a compromise is still possible, but a credit of confidence without any guarantees is not. The need for much deeper change has been made apparent to all.

A reform in policy would, however, be constrained by ' Poland's membership of the Warsaw Pact and by the Soviet military presence. Would the USSR permit any great changes to take place? There is a factor which both the Soviet and Polish leaderships and also the democratic opposition have in common: for each of the three, Soviet military intervention would be a catastrophe. One should, however, not preclude the possibility of such an intervention. It might even be inevitable should the Soviet and Polish Governments on the one hand and the people of Poland on the other lose their sense of reality and proportion, or just their common-sense. As for the democratic opposition, they should bear in mind the limits of possible reform. And, last but not least, the Party leadership should understand that in opting for repression against rebellious workers and students they are digging their own grave.

During the June events the fictitious nature of the official trade unions was once again demonstrated. It is evident today that without the independent representation of the workers, comparable, say, to the worker-councils in Spain, there can be no durable compromise between the authorities and the people. Only a representation of this kind would allow for the defence of workers' interests and for a resolution of social tensions without bloodshed. It is not realistic to suppose that there are no conflicts within Polish society. The alternative way leads to totalitarianism, to bloody confrontation and brings public opprobrium on the government.

There is also a need for reformation of relations between the Church and State. In Poland Catholics are treated as second class citizens. This injustice is inadmissible; as is the imposition of the official atheism. Catholics should have the right to play a part in public life, as demanded by Cardinal Wyszyński. There should also be greater freedom to publish books on religious subjects.

Problem of censorship

This is where the problem of censorship comes in. The senseless use of preventive censorship must be changed. I admit that, for the moment, it is unrealistic to wish this institution to be purely and simply abolished; but the present state of affairs in which the censor's pencil has the right to delimit political and intellectual horizons, cannot continue indefinitely. If the authorities continue to destroy the intellectual life of Poland, they can only compel the writers to publish their work either abroad or in *samizdat* form.

A reasonable law to regulate the press which would legalize censorship — an institution at present illegal — in certain areas, and suppress it in others would be the solution. It is difficult to justify preventive censorship of low-circulation philosophical or literary journals or specialized periodicals. In this area preventive measures could be replaced by simple regulations of the kind that exist for example in Yugoslavia. The mass media, also subject to censorship, should make room for simple political reporting; their sole function should not be to bolster Party and State officials, while people listen to Radio Free Europe or other Western transmissions for the information they want. Western literature, including emigré works, must be allowed in Poland, in compliance with the Helsinki agreement.

In addition the Party leaders would do well to renounce their aspirations to quell pluralism among young people. The young, and students in particular, should have the legal right to form independent academic societies and clubs. By denying them this right the authorities are compelling them to illegal action and themselves shoulder responsibility for the violation of the law on this matter.

All these issues seem to me to be important, and important not for the Poles alone. To a certain extent the fate of Europe depends on the situation prevailing in Poland: the existence of implacable totalitarianism in one part of the continent must threaten the continuation of democracy in the other. Public opinion in Europe, and especially that of the left, is of considerable significance; the Poles ask for no more than moral support from the West. To refuse them that for the sake of currying favour with the Party *élites* of Eastern Europe is to help to maintain in those countries attitudes which one can only describe as reactionary.

Détente in Europe is in all respects a positive concept; it permits political realism. That being so, however, there is no reason for self-congratulation for the system that rules in Warsaw. There is one other approach, one well known to the French Left, which is contained in the words: "Vive la Pologne!".

THE MOVEMENT FOR HUMAN AND CIVIL RIGHTS TO THE PEOPLE OF POLAND

On 25 March 1977, a new opposition group representing a somewhat different political stance (leaning towards right rather than left) was set up in Poland: The Movement for the Defence of Human and Civil Rights (MDHCR), with the principle concern of checking on the genuine implementation of human rights in Poland. In its aim it thus does not compete with the Workers' Defence Committee which came into being specifically to deal with the aftermath of the food price disturbances. As if to stress the compatibility of the two bodies, three members of the WDC (Pajdak, Rev. Zieja and Ziembiński) signed the MDCHR's founding document (page 182) along with 15 other people.

The MDHCR was within days opening Information and Consultation Centres at the homes of its members and so was in some ways pre-empting the WDC's decision to organize a Bureau for Interventions (see page 143) after the death of Pyjas in mid-May.

Initially, the MDHCR confined itself to issuing statements on matters of public concern (such as the temporary detention in mid-April of a number of WDC members, the death of Pyjas, the longer-term arrests of WDC members and collaborators) and also to gathering further information on the abuses of human rights.

On 30 April, the Movement initiated the publication of a journal Opinion, which has, since then, appeared on an almost monthly basis. Issue No. 4, dated 1 August, stated on the first page that "2,500 copies were run off and the combined effects of more than 100 people were responsible for this production".* It contained information about the WDC, abuses of human rights, actions of the authorities not reported by the media, and a series of articles analysing various aspects of the Polish economy. One short note read as follows:

"The MDHCR is making visible progress as more and more people help it in its work. [Membership was at this point reckoned at about 800.] In addition to the three existing Information and Consultation Centres, two new ones have been opened. They are thus, at the moment, operating in Katowice, Łódź, Poznań, Przemyśl and Warsaw. There is a systematic growth in the activity of the regional groups in all the larger Polish towns as well as in the smaller ones and in rural areas. The regional groups in Gdańsk and Lublin have been especially dynamic. A number of groups are preparing papers on specific aspects of human and civil rights."

Despite the declared intentions of the instigators of the MDHCR, there has been friction between them and the WDC. To some extent, this is due to their ideological differences (simplifying greatly, most of the leading personalities in the WDC tend to be left of centre, while in the MDCHR they tend to be right of centre).

Recently (29 September 1977) the WDC transformed itself into the Committee for Social Self-Defence. Three of the original WDC members dropped out; Ziembiński wished to devote himself much more to Opinion (he is one of its three editors), while Morgiewicz had close links with Czuma (both were imprisoned for their involvement in the clandestine organization "Ruch"). Obviously it is in the interests of the authorities to exacerbate relations between the two groups and both groups are well aware of this. It would be a tragedy if conflicts and distrust were to arise, since the existence of these two organizations may be seen as the beginning of democratic pluralism. Moreover, many young people .frighten them; are involved on both sides. The murder of Pyjas did not on the contrary, the number of young WDC collaborators doubled after

---

* The appearance of samizdat journals with relatively large circulation is a new and growing phenomenon. Other journals came into existence during 1977; for example, U progu (On the threshold) anticipated Opinion by a few months, while Robotnik (The Worker) was started up by some WDC members in September; a further journal Głos (Voice) appeared in October (this one ran to 77 pages and, according to its editors, had a circulation of 1000).

that tragic event. In committing themselves in this way, they too have broken through the barriers of fear and in so doing have made it very difficult for the authorities to react with the usual reprisals.

MOVEMENT FOR THE DEFENCE OF HUMAN AND CIVIL RIGHTS IN POLAND

On 10th December 1948 the United Nations General Assembly passed the Universal Declaration of Human Rights. This document codified the key provisions with regard to the defence, freedom and dignity of the individual. As a result, respect for fundamental human liberties became an intrinsic part of the contemporary and future order in the world. Consolidation of the principle in the world community was given expression on 16th December 1966, when the U.N. General Assembly passed the International Pacts on Human Rights, which have the stature of International Law, binding those states which ratified the pacts. They came into effect at the beginning of 1976, after ratification by the required number of 35 countries; in the Polish People's Republic they are binding from 3rd March 1977, i.e. from the moment of their ratification.

We accept with satisfaction the ratification of the Pacts on Human Rights by the Council of State in Poland and believe it to be in agreement with the fundamental desires of the people of Poland.

It is one of the most valuable and ever-thriving traditions of the Polish nation that great importance is attached to the rights of man and of the citizen, to the dignity of the individual, to freedom and mutual tolerance. Over the centuries these fundamental principles have found expression in such documents as *Neminem Captivabimus, Nihil Novi,* the Warsaw Confederacy, the Constitution of 3rd May, and in the historic motto "For Your Freedom and Ours"; having been for many generations a quintessential part of our national consciousness, they are generally accepted to be indispensable to our life as a society.

For this reason we affirm, together with other peoples of the world: — that human and civil rights are inviolable and inalienable; they can not be relinquished. No nation can be truly free if its members renounce the use and defence of their own rights, as historical experience, including that of the Poles, has shown.

— Whereas respect, and demand for respect, for human rights and dignity belongs to the most valuable traditions and achievements of Polish culture

— whereas the fundamental guarantees of the freedom and dignity of the individual as defined in the Universal Declaration of Human Rights and the International Pacts on Human Rights are generally accepted today to be one of the key attainments of our civilisation

— whereas the Final Act of the Conference on Security and Co-operation in Europe, signed on 31st July 1975 in Helsinki binds all the signatory states to act in accordance with the aims and principles of the Charters of the United Nations and the Universal Declaration of Human Rights, raising respect for the rights and liberties of the individual, as there defined, to the status of a factor controlling international relations on our continent,

— whereas the Constitution of the Polish People's Republic also affirms the implementation of the civil liberties contained in the Universal Declaration of Human Rights, such as: freedom of conscience, of the spoken and written word, of demonstration, of meeting and association, and that the practical realisation of these provisions has become indispensable not only for the spiritual welfare of our country, but also because it is a *sine qua non* for the expansion of our economy and culture,

therefore, we, the undersigned, have decided to take up joint action in order to:

1. Adhere to, and watch for compliance with, all human and civil rights and the principle of human dignity;
2. Make known to public opinion and to the appropriate authorities any infringements on human rights and liberties, and to provide victims with such assistance and protection as lies within our scope;
3. Propagate among the public and propose to the State Authorities changes in the law and regulations which would lead to a genuine and continuous assurance of the implementation of the rights and liberties defined in the Universal Declaration of Human Rights and the International Pacts on Human Rights;
4. Propagate the need for all European countries to be party to the International Pacts on Human Rights, in order to create a common legal and political base for the development of genuine détente and understanding in Europe;

5. Co-operate with all international organisations which defend human rights, and with the U.N. Human Rights Commission in particular, so that the principle of freedom may triumph in the world.

We are not forming an organisation or association. Our initiative is the result of urgent public need.

A strong social current is already manifest in Poland — a movement in defence of Human and Civil Rights.

We appeal to everyone in Poland for moral support, for co-operation and help, particularly in obtaining essential information concerning the infringement of human and civil rights; we appeal to everyone to take up and expand similar initiatives in all social, professional and regional millieux. Human and civil rights and the dignity of the individual can be preserved only when they are respected by all, and all actively demand that they be respected.

Compiled on 25th March 1977

— General Mieczysław BORUTA-SPIECHOWICZ, the most senior in rank of soldiers of the 2nd Republic (inter-war Poland) living in Poland; Zakopane, ul. Szymanowskiego 16

— Andrzej CZUMA, lawyer, former political prisoner; Włochy nr. Warsaw, ul. Jagny 11 — tel. 23 75 91

— Karol GŁOGOWSKI, lawyer, the organiser and leader of the Association of Young Democrats in 1956-57; Łódź, ul. Chanocka 24 m. 61 — tel. 462 10

— Kazimierz JANUSZ, engineer, former political prisoner; Warsaw, ul. Czerniakowska 34 m. 120 — tel. 40 01 80

— Stefan KACZOROWSKI, lawyer, formerly a Christian democratic activist and member of the Polish Resistance; Łódź, ul. Bednarska 9 m. 114 — tel. 452 20

— Leszek MOCZULSKI, writer and historian; Warsaw, ul. Jaracza 2 m. 23 — tel. 26 26 39

— Marek MYSZKIEWICZ-NIESIOŁOWSKI, mechanical engineer, former political prisoner; Łódź, ul. Armii Czerwonej 7 m. 2

— Antoni PAJDAK, lawyer, former Polish Socialist Party activist, one of the leaders of the Polish Resistance; Warsaw, Śliska 10 m. 76

— Rev. Bogdan PAPIERNIK, Łódź, ul. Św. Antoniego 1

— Zbigniew SEKULSKI, sociologist, social worker; Łódź, ul. Sporna 16

— Zbigniew SIEMIŃSKI, Polish scholar, social worker; Łódź, ul. Lanowa 113 m. 5

— Bogumił STUDZIŃSKI, lawyer, social worker; Zalesie Górne nr. Warsaw, ul. Złocistych Łanów 27 — tel. 56 53 16

— Piotr STYPIAK, former People's Movement and Polish Resistance activist; Warsaw, ul. Łowicka 53 — tel. 49 03 86

— Rev. Ludwik WIŚNIEWSKI, Dominican priest; Lublin, ul. Złota 9 — tel. 289 80

— Adam WOJCIECHOWSKI, lawyer, member of Amnesty International; Warsaw, ul. Ordynacka 10/12 m. 18 — tel. 26 95 11

— Andrzej WOŹNICKI, chemist, former political prisoner; Łódź, ul. Rydlowa 17

— Rev. Jan ZIEJA, former chaplain to the Polish Army and the "Grey Ranks" of the Home Army (Resistance); Warsaw, ul. Dobra 59 m. 13

— Wojciech ZIEMBIŃSKI, editor, social worker; Warsaw, ul. Sady Żoliborskie 7 a m. 21 — tel. 33 05 46

The release of the above statement met with a virulent attack by Trybuna Ludu, the Party daily. The editor-in-chief, J. Barecki, accused the Movement of being anti-Polish and "blindly servile to foreign anti-Communist centres". He described the appeal for information on alleged human rights violations in Poland as "a manifestation of ill-will, an outright falsification and an act of political damage". It was in the West, he explained, and not in Poland that human rights were violated. Barecki justified this view by pointing out that Poland had been especially active at the U.N. in the field of human rights.

THE MDHCR ignored this and in mid-April issued the following laconic message:

PRESS RELEASE

.... Warsaw, 15th April 1977

On 15th April 1977 the first two Consultation and Information Centres of the Movement for the Defence of Human and Civil Rights were opened in Warsaw and Łódź.

The Warsaw Consultation and Information Centre is open on Mondays and Fridays between 16.30 and 18.30 hrs., at the home of Mr Kazimierz JANUSZ, ul. Czerniakowska 34 m. 120, telephone no. 40 01 80.

The Łódź Consultation and Information Centre is open on Wednesdays from 17.00 to 19.00 hrs., at the home of Mr Benedykt CZUMA, ul. Konstytucyjna 11 m. 1, near 3rd May Park, telephone no. 868 57.

The Consultation and Information Centres receive Citizens' comments and proposals regarding the implementation of human, and civil rights in Poland; they also provide information and legal advice.

Andrzej CZUMA and Leszek MOCZULSKI
Spokesmen for the Movement for the
Defence of Human and Civil Rights

BIOGRAPHICAL NOTES

JERZY ANDRZEJEWSKI A widely acclaimed author of, amongst others, the book "Ashes and Diamonds". In 1968, sent a letter to the president of the Association of Czechoslovak Writers expressing solidarity with the Czech and Slovak writers and condemning the invasion of Czechoslovakia by Warsaw Pact forces. One of the signatories of the memorable "Letter of the 34" in March 1964, protesting against the limitations imposed on cultural freedom. In 1971 signed a protest memorandum against the judgements passed at the trials of the members of the clandestine organization "Ruch".

STEFAN AMSTERDAMSKI. One time Head of the Philosophy Department in the Faculty of History and Philosophy at the University of Łódź. Removed from the Party and dismissed from his acdaemic post in the antisemitic campaign of 1968. Sympathized with the students during the March demonstrations of 1968.

STANISŁAW BARAŃCZAK. Well-known poet, author and young literary critic.

WŁADYSŁAW BIEŃKOWSKI. Minister of Education (1956–59) in the Gomułka government. Since falling from grace has enjoyed considerable freedom of expression. Wrote two books for the Polish emigré publishing house "Institut Littéraire" (Paris).

JACEK BIEREZIN. Young poet who has lately enjoyed exceptional popularity. Arrested in 1970 for belonging to the underground organisation "Ruch". In 1971 in Łódź, proceedings were taken against him in one of the trials of the organisation's members. Subjected to various acts of repression after the publication by the emigré "Institut Littéraire" in Paris of a volume of his poems (which had earlier been rejected by the censors in Poland). Prevented from continuing his studies at the University of Łódź.

KAZIMIERZ BRANDYS. Writer and essayist. In 1966 left the Party in protest against the repressions which befell Professor Leszek Kołakowski. One of the signatories of the protest memorandum against the judgements passed at the trials of the members of "Ruch", and also signed the letter to the Minister of Culture of the Polish People's Republic about the fate of Poles held in Russia.

MARIAN BRANDYS. Writer and author of some very popular historical novels.

BOHDAN CHWEDEŃCZUK. Lecturer at the University of Warsaw and close associate of Professor Leszek Kołakowski. In 1968, barred

187

from the University during the purge by the Party on academics accused of instigating the March student demonstrations.

LUDWIK COHN. *Before the Second World War was active in the Polish Socialist Party. Took part in the Polish Campaign in 1939 and was later imprisoned in German concentration camps. In October 1947 was sentenced to 5 years' imprisonment by the communist powers in the trial of the leader of the Polish Socialists, Kazimierz Pużak and of other members of an anti-Nazi underground organization.*

IRENA EICHLERÓWNA. *Popular film and theatre actress.*

STANISŁAW GAJEWSKI. *For many years a distinguished member of the diplomatic service. In the years 1954–61, was the Ambassador of the Polish People's Republic in Paris and later became the director of the Department for Western Affairs in the Ministry of Foreign Affairs.*

PROF. WACŁAW GAJEWSKI. *Lecturer at the University of Warsaw, a well-known geneticist and for many years the director of the Institute of Biochemistry and Biophysics at the Polish Academy of Sciences.*

PROF. ANDRZEJ GRZEGORCZYK. *A logician working in the Institute of Philosophy and Sociology at the Polish Academy of Sciences.*

ZBIGNIEW HERBERT. *World-famous poet, essayist and author of many works for stage and radio. In 1965 was the recipient of the Austrian Nicholas Lenau Award for his outstanding achievements in the realm of European literary works. In November 1971, together with Wiktor Woroszylski, was the main instigator of the protest of the 18 writers against the judgements passed at the political trials of the underground group "Ruch".*

RYSZARD HERCZYNSKI. *Applied Mathematician working for the Institute of Basic Technical Research (Polish Academy of Sciences). In 1967 bravely and publicly voiced his opposition against repressions that befell Professor Leszek Kołakowski.*

MARYLA HOPFINGER. *Literary critic at the Literary Institute of the Polish Academy of Sciences, Warsaw. Wife of Stefan Amsterdamski. In 1966, together with six other academics, signed a letter to the editor of "Pravda" protesting against the harsh judgements passed against the Russian writers Daniel and Sinyavsky.*

REV. KRZYSZTOF KASZNICA. *Dominican and former Provincial of the Dominican Fathers in Poland.*

PROF. JAN KIELANOWSKI. *Former soldier of the Polish Underground Home Army. Active member of the Polish Academy of Sciences. For many years the director of the Institute of Physiology and Animal Husbandry near Warsaw. In 1975 was awarded an honorary doctorate by the University of St. Andrews in Scotland.*

ANDRZEJ KIJOWSKI. *Essayist, writer and literary critic. At the memorable extraordinary meeting of the Warsaw Branch of the Association of Polish Writers in February 1968, presented a resolution con- protest of 18 writers against the judgements passed at the trials of "Ruch", and in 1974 signed a petition to the Minister of Culture of*

188

demning the activities of the censors. In 1971, was a signatory of the the Polish People's Republic regarding the fate of Poles held in Russia. *STEFAN KISIELEWSKI.* Widely known writer, publicist, musicologist, newspaper columnist and former Member of the Parliament of the Polish People's Republic. One of the 34 signatories of the famous memorandum of March 1964, written in protest against censorship and the limitations of cultural freedom. Joint author of the resolution passed at the General Meeting of the Warsaw Branch of the Literary Association in February 1968, which protested against the banning of the play "Dziady" ("Forefathers") from the stage of the National Theatre. More than once personally criticized by the communist leadership, for example by Gomułka in 1969. Severely beaten by security agents during the student demonstrations of 1968.

PROF. LESZEK KOŁAKOWSKI. World-famous Marxist philosopher, a former lecturer in philosophy and social studies at the Institute of Social Studies. Expelled from the Party in 1966 for voicing so-called "revisionist" views. One of the initiators behind the convening of the extraordinary meeting of the Warsaw Branch of the Association of Polish Writers in February 1968 in connection with the removal of the play "Dziady" ("Forefathers") from the stage at the National Theatre. In March 1968 was deprived of the Chair of Philosophy at the University of Warsaw. On many occasions was criticized publicly by the Gomułka and Party propagandists as one of the principal instigators of the March student demonstrations.

JULIAN KORNHAUSER. Poet, author and outstanding exponent of the new trends in Polish poetry.

MARIA KORNIŁOWICZ. Grand-daughter of writer and Nobel prizewinner Henryk Sienkiewicz. Writer and translator of literature from French and English.

WŁADYSŁAW KUNICKI-GOLDFINGER. Eminent biologist. For many years a lecturer at the Universities in Wrocław and Warsaw. A member of the Polish Academy of Sciences, working at the Institute of Microbiology in the University of Warsaw.

JACEK KUROŃ. In March 1964, whilst a postgraduate student at the Institute of Education (Warsaw), wrote, together with Karol Modzelewski, the famous "Open Letter" to the Party strongly criticizing conditions in Poland. Arrested as a result, and later expelled from the Party in December 1964, he was sentenced to 3 years' imprisonment on the charge of disseminating material ostensibly "harmful to the nation's interests". Re-arrested in March 1968 and sentenced to $3\frac{1}{2}$ years' imprisonment as one of those accused of instigating the March student demonstrations. Criticised publicly on many occasions by Gomułka and Party propagandists. In 1975 signed the letter from five young lecturers expressing support for and recognition of Professor Andrei Sakharov, the recipient of the Nobel Peace Prize.

ZDZISŁAW ŁAPIŃSKI. Doctor of medicine and outstanding professor of the Medical Academy in Warsaw. Treasurer of the Federation of Polish Medical Societies.

PROF. EDWARD LIPIŃSKI. The most eminent Polish economist, author of over 200 educational works, which have been translated into many European languages. For many years a lecturer at the Central School of Planning and Statistics, and President of the Polish Economics Society. In 1959, was decorated by the régime with the Order of the Banner of Labour (1st class). In 1964 was the signatory of the famous letter from 34 intellectuals which opposed censorship and limitations of cultural freedom. In 1973 was the recipient of the Oskar Lange Award from the Polish Economics Society for his work "Karl Marx and present-day problems". Also a signatory of the letter by 15 intellectuals directed to the Minister of Culture of the Polish People's Republic in 1974 demanding that Poles held in Russia be given the rights to which national minorities are entitled.

JAN JÓZEF LIPSKI. Master of Philosophy. Former soldier of the Polish Underground Home Army. Writer and literary critic. Arrested many times for his bold stand against censorship, including in 1964 for collecting signatures for the famous "Letter of the 34" which expressed opposition against the cultural policies in Poland.

PROF. JERZY ŁOŚ. Mathematician. For many years a professor at the Nicholas Copernicus University in Toruń. A member of the Polish Academy of Sciences, working in the Institute of Mathematics, now at the Computing Centre of the Polish Academy of Sciences. Important contributions to Logic and Mathematical Economics.

REV. STANISŁAW MAŁKOWSKI. Well-known sociologist and authority on the problems of delinquency.

JERZY MARKUSZEWSKI. Well-known theatrical producer, one of the founders of the famous Students' Theatre of Satire. For many years worked in television.

ADAM MICHNIK. As an undergraduate rallied students at Warsaw University in support of the release of Kuroń and Modzelewski. Also involved (January 1968) in collecting signatures under a petition protesting against the banning of "Dziady" ("Forefathers' Eve") at the National Theatre. Suspended several times by the University, was eventually sent down (on the decision of the Minister of Education) in May 1968. This caused further student unrest. The following year sentenced to 3 years' imprisonment and condemned by the Communist Party press as being one of the organizers of the March student demonstrations. Subjected to preventive arrest during the visit of President Nixon to Warsaw in 1972 and during the collecting of signatures in 1974 for the petition by 15 intellectuals regarding Poles in Russia. In 1975 was one of the signatiries of the letter of five young lecturers expressing recognition for Professor Sakharov. Visited the West in late 1976 and early 1977 where he appealed for support for the Polish dissidents, to Western Public opinion, in a series of articles and interviews.

HALINA MIKOŁAJSKA. Excellent and widely-acclaimed theatre and film actress.

190

JAN NEPOMUCEN MILLER. Poet, literary critic and prominent socialist writer. During the occupation of Poland in the Second World War was the co-author of an underground paper of the Polish Socialists. For many years was the president of the Warsaw Branch of the Association of Polish Writers. One of the signatories of the petition by 15 intellectuals about Poles in Russia.

WOJCIECH MŁYNARSKI. Popular singer and author of many satyrical texts and protest songs.

ZOFIA MROZOWSKA. Theatre and film actress. For many years the Dean of the Drama Department at the National Advanced School of Theatre in Warsaw. In 1970, decorated with the Cross of the Order of Polonia Restituta for her services in the field of culture.

ZYGMUNT MYCIELSKI. World-famous composer, musicologist, essayist and editor. Harassed by the régime for the publishing of an open letter, in the Autumn of 1968 in the Paris newspaper Le Monde, protesting against the invasion of Czechoslovakia by the Warsaw Pact troops. In 1974 signed a letter to the Minister of Culture of the Polish People's Republic demanding the rights of Poles held in the Soviet Union.

ZDZISŁAW NAJDER. Writer and literary critic working at the Institute of Literary Research and member of the editorial team of the monthly "Twórczość" ("Creativity"). Expert on the works of Joseph Conrad and the editor of the first edition of the complete works by this writer.

JAN OLSZEWSKI. Lawyer, well-known publicist, member of the famous editorial team during October 1956 of the weekly "Po Prostu" ("Quite Simply"). Has appeared as Counsel for the Defence in many famous political trials and because of this has been subject to harassment, including suspension from practising as a lawyer and being taken to court and sentenced to 8 months' imprisonment.

KAZIMIERZ ORŁOŚ. Talented writer of the younger generation. Following disciplinary proceedings, was removed from the editorial team of the Polish Radio's literature section and from the editorial team of the weekly "Literatura" ("Literature"), for the publishing of one of his books in 1973 by the emigré "Institut Littéraire" in Paris.

ANTONI PAJDAK. 86 year old veteran of the Polish Workers' Movement. A well-known pre-war member of the Polish Socialist Party. A former soldier of the Polish Underground Home Army. In 1945 tricked into being arrested by the NKVD (Soviet secret police) and taken to Moscow. Sentenced to the labour camps for 5 years in the famous trial of the 16 leaders of the Polish Underground.

ANNA PAWEŁCZYŃSKA. Reader, assistant professor, sociologist, authoress and for many years the director of the Public Opinion Research Centre with the Polish Radio. A member of the Institute of Philosophy and Sociology at the Polish Academy of Sciences.

KRZYSZTOF POMIAN. Former assistant lecturer at the University of Warsaw and one of Prof. Kołakowski's closest associates. Dismissed from the Party following disciplinary proceedings in 1966 because of his bold criticisms of the conditions prevailing in Poland. In June 1968, together with other members of the University of Warsaw, signed a letter to the Moscow paper "Pravda" protesting against the judgements passed against the Russian writers Daniel and Sinyavsky. Dismissed from the University of Warsaw in 1968 and officially condemned as one of the leading lights of the March student demonstrations. Has been subject to constant harassment by the régime and has been denied the possibility of freely continuing his academic activities. Now in the West.

REV. JACEK SALIJ. Dominican. Students' Chaplain at the Catholic University of Lublin, particularly popular amongst young people. Organizer of student gatherings, for which he is being harassed by the security agents.

WŁADYSŁAW SIŁA-NOWICKI. Pre-war Workers' Party activist. Eminent lawyer and Defence Counsel in many famous political trials including that of Nina Karsov and those of students accused of organising demonstrations in March 1968. Barred from practising his profession and tried for the possession of "illegal" literature.

COL. STANISŁAW SKALSKI. Highly decorated "flying ace" of the Polish Air Force during the Second World War, who distinguished himself in the Battle of Britain in 1940. Holder of many Polish and foreign decorations, was twice decorated with the highest national award, the Virtuti Militari (IV and V class) and also awarded the Cross of the Order Polonia Restituta. Returned to Poland in 1947 and a year later was arrested. In April 1950 was sentenced to death by a military tribunal. The sentence was commuted, after countless appeals, to life imprisonment, and later still to 12 years in jail. In October 1956 was released from prison, rehabilitated and accepted into active service in the Air Force. For many years a general secretary of the Polish Aeroclub and also of the Association of Fighters for Liberty and Democracy.

ALEKSANDRA ŚLĄSKA. Highly acclaimed theatre, film and television actress. In 1974 was the recipient of the award "Złoty Ekran" ("Golden Screen") from the weekly "Ekran" ("Screen") for the best creative acting.

ANTONI SŁONIMSKI. Senior Polish writer, excellent poet, essayist and columnist. One of the most uncompromising critics of censorship and a signatory of the memorable "letter of 34" in March 1964, protesting against the limitations in cultural freedom. One of the signatories also of the letter from 15 intellectuals concerning Poles in Russia. Died 4 July 1976 as a result of a car accident.

DR. ADAM STANOWSKI. Young Catholic educationalist, publicist and lecturer at the Department of Christian Philosophy in the Catholic University of Lublin.

ANIELA STEINSBERGOWA. Pre-war member of the Polish Socialist Party, a lawyer by profession. Has acted as Defence Counsel in numer-

ous political trials, including that of Jacek Kuroń and Karol Modze-
lewski in 1966. Subjected to harassment by the régime, and for her
activities barred from practising her profession.

JULIAN STRYJKOWSKI. *Pre-war communist activist. Well-known*
writer, essayist, literary critic and translator of French and Russian
literature. In 1966 signed a protest letter against the expulsion of Prof.
Kołakowski from the Party.

PROF. STEFAN ŚWIEŻAWSKI. *Holder of the Chair of Mediaeval*
and Modern Philosophy at the Catholic University of Lublin.

JAN JÓZEF SZCZEPAŃSKI. *Took part in the Polish Campaign, 1939.*
Well-known author of many literary works including film scripts, director
of the literary theatre "Groteska" in Cracow and a committee member
of the Association of Polish Writers.

ADAM SZCZYPIORSKI. *80 year old professor, doctor of philosophy*
and pre-war activist of the Polish Socialist Party. Father of the well-
known writer and publicist Andrzej Szczypiorski.

KAZIMIERZ SZELĄGOWSKI. *Professor and highly-acclaimed educa-*
tionalist. Member of the resistance movement in Poland during the
occupation in the Second World War. After the war in 1945–47 was
Consul of the Polish People's Republic in Belgium. For many years
a lecturer in the Institute of Foreign Languages.

WISŁAWA SZYMBORSKA. *Outstanding poetess and translator of*
French and German literature. Authoress of many collections of poetry.
In 1963 received an award from the Ministry of Culture and Arts for
one of her volumes of poetry. Left the Party in 1966 in protest against
the repressions which befell Prof. Kołakowski. Still lives in Cracow and
is a committee member of the Association of Polish Writers.

KRYSTYNA TARNAWSKA. *Well-known translator of literature from*
English speaking nations. During the occupation of Poland in the Second
World War, served in the Polish Underground Home Army. A former
inmate of the notorious Pawiak Prison and Nazi concentration camps.

WANDA WIŁKOMIRSKA. *Violinist of world repute, a soloist of the*
National Philharmonic Orchestra and the Grand Orchestra of the Polish
Radio. In 1964 was decorated with the Order of the Banner of Labour
(1st class).

WIKTOR WOROSZYLSKI. *Brilliant poet, essayist, publicist and writer.*
The author of the monumental work entitled "Życie Majakowskiego"
("The Life of Majakowski"). Dismissed from the Party in 1967 following
disciplinary proceedings for being associated with the acts of protests
against the repressions which befell Professor Kołakowski. In 1971 was
one of the initiators of the protest by 18 writers against the judgements
passed at the political trials of the underground organization "Ruch"
In 1974, was a signatory of the petition by 15 intellectuals concerning
the fate of Poles held in the Soviet Union.

PROF. KAZIMIERZ ZAKRZEWSKI. *Eminent biochemist, Assistant*
Professor at the Polish Academy of Sciences and for many years an
adviser to the United Nations Commission dealing with research into

13*

atomic radiation. A director of the biochemical works at the Institute of Haematology. An associate member of the New York Academy of Science, Professor at the Institute of Nuclear Research in Świersk, near Warsaw, and chairman of the Federation of European Biochemical Societies.

REV. JAN ZIEJA. During the occupation of Poland in the Second World War was Chaplain of the Polish Underground Home Army. Organizer of the Catholic Intelligentsia Clubs and patron of the Institute for the Blind near Warsaw. In 1954 arrested for protesting against the imprisonment of Cardinal Wyszyński. Widely known as a result of his many stirring sermons regarding the enslavement of Poland. A signatory of the memorandum from 15 intellectuals regarding the rights of Poles held in the Soviet Union.

SELECTED CHRONOLOGY
June 1976–June 1977

25 June. Worker demonstrations over food price rises; the Ursus factory at Warsaw and the population of Radom especially affected; price rises rescinded.

29 June. Letter of the 14 to Sejm (Polish Parliament); 14 intellectuals call for "authentic dialogue" between government and people.

11 July. Jacek Kuroń, dissident intellectual, sends open letter to Enrico Berlinguer of the Italian Communist Party, appeals for support against "massive repression" of workers; Kuroń reports widespread dismissals of those involved in demonstrations.

Mid-July. Cardinal Stefan Wyszyński sent a private letter to the Polish Prime Minister, Piotr Jaroszewicz, asking for toleration and for an end to arrests and interrogations of workers.

19 July. Group of workers from Radom receive heavy sentences on charges of criminal activities.

20 July. Group of workers from Ursus receive somewhat lighter sentences. Italian CP sends message to Polish Party, expressing the hope that moderation will prevail and that clemency will be shown. "It must be possible in socialist countries to resolve social disagreements and even conflicts without serious disturbances."

29 July. Polish government spokesman, Włodzimierz Janiurek, denied Western reports that 17 people had been killed during the disturbances in Radom, but admitted that 53 people had been sentenced.

9 August. The newspaper *Życie Warszawy* reported more trials at Radom and Ursus on charges of hooliganism.

3 Sept. Edward Gierek, Polish party leader, made a speech at Mielec; positive on Church-State relations and implied that problems in this area could be resolved.

9 Sept. 154th Plenary Conference of the Polish Episcopate met at Częstochowa; communiqué expressed deep concern over the unrest in the country; appealed to government to respect civic rights and to people "to preserve domestic peace and order". Also called for an amnesty for those imprisoned and for compensation for loss of earnings.

23 Sept. A human rights lawyer, Aniela Steinsbergowa, sent an "Appeal to the Nation and the Authorities of the People's Republic of Poland" on behalf of the newly formed Workers' Defence Committee, a private group. The appeal asked for an investigation into police brutality against the workers.

26 Sept. Wyszyński's sermon stated that it was "painful when workers must struggle for their rights from a workers government"; he reminded the bishops that they must remember their duties to the working people — this move was interpreted as tacit support for the Committee (WDC) by the Church, an institution of great authority in Poland.

27 Sept. Supreme Court reduced Ursus sentences from 5 to 3 years to 1 year suspended. This concession to Polish opinion received very little publicity in the official media. The WDC made a public announcement of its existence, It comprised 15 members, notably the writer Jerzy Andrzejewski, and it issued a protest against police brutality. It stated that 160,000 zlotys had been collected on behalf of the dependants of those arrested. The WDC's first communiqué contained a full list of the names and adresses of its members and was released to Western correspondents.

10 Oct. WDC communiqué on its activities noted that 73 workers had been sentenced at Radom; 250,000 zlotys spent on dependants, some 98 families were in receipt of relief; total number of workers sacked was probably about 1000. Members of the WDC were being subjected to harassment by the authorities.

12 Oct. New list of complaints against police and appeal issued by Władysław Bieńkowski (text in Index on Censorship, January–February 1977, p. 52) on the same subject. Edward Gierek's speech at Katowice attacked "internal allies" of "reactionary cold war forces abroad", an implicit reference to the WDC.

30 Oct. WDC's 3rd communiqué: membership up to 18; "verified cases" of 11 deaths at Radom, contradicting official account of two deaths; money still being collected, at times openly; protest against a false "Communiqué No. 3", a secret police fabrication aimed at discrediting the WDC; harassment of members continued.

4 Nov. Letter sent by 889 Ursus workers calling on Gierek to reinstate those who had been sacked.

16 Nov. WDC again asked Sejm to investigate police brutality.

18 Nov. Polish bishops at the 155th Episcopal Conference called for an amnesty for workers, noted that their earlier appeal had been ignored and announced that aid was being given to dependants at the parish level. Janiurek criticised Western media for the way in which Polish affairs were being reported; declared that the WDC was illegal under a precommunist law of 1932; and added that only "intellectual" methods would be used against WDC members.

22 Nov. WDC's 4th communiqué: 658,000 zlotys had been disbursed; the disturbances in June had been much more widespread than originally reported — there had been unrest at Łódź, Gdańsk, Szczecin, Elbląg and elsewhere, at all these places workers had been dismissed; there had also been some reinstatements.

23 Nov. Detention of 14 WDC members by police for questioning; house searches and confiscation of documents.

24 Nov. Sakharov expresses support for WDC.

28 Nov. An Episcopal Letter, in answer to Gierek's Mielec speech, released. It contained a long list of the issues that separated Church and State.

1 Dec. Meeting of the Polish Party's Central Committee; Gierek attempted to discredit the WDC, though not by name, by linking it with West German revanchism.

1 Dec. 67 workers appeal for the establishment of a Sejm commission to investigate police brutality; supported by Bieńkowski; dependants of imprisoned workers testify to police brutality.

5 Dec. Card. Wyszyński made strong attack on the authorities, charging them with condoning police brutality. He gave his backing to un-official collecting of money for aid to dependants.

9 Dec. The dissident historian Adam Michnik gave a press conference in London, details of police behaviour; outlined the ideas of the op-position, which he said was working for the eventual "Finlandization of Poland".

11 Dec. Supreme Court confirmed some sentences and reduced others passed on Radom workers.

13 Dec. The party daily *Trybuna Ludu* made the first official attack on the WDC by name; it described them as "opponents of socialism", and as actuated by "revisionism" and "neo-positivism" (i.e., Roman Catholic ideas). The WDC welcomed this official acknowledgement of its existence.

14 Dec. Interviewed in the *Financial Times*, Jaroszewicz said that nobody was "now in jail because of participation in the strikes"; he described the WDC as something to laugh at.

17 Dec. Attacks on WDC and particularly on Jerzy Andrzejewski continue; also accused of Zionism.

20 Dec. Continuing harassment of WDC members reported.

21 Dec. 28 intellectuals, academics sent letter to Sejm, called for investigation of police behaviour.

1977

4 Jan. The WDC again called on the Sejm to investigate allegations of police brutality.

5 Jan. Answering before Sejm Committee on Internal Affairs, the Procurator General denied that any police brutality had taken place.

6 Jan. An appeal signed by 172 intellectuals, writers, actors etc., many of them well known, called on the authorities to establish the Sejm Commission of Inquiry.

9 Jan. *Życie Warszawy* published another attack on the WDC (though not by name) and on Andrzejewski; it warned that their activities were not in the interests of the nation and that limits of treason to the nation were indistinct.

16 Jan. Supreme Court reduced sentences on 6 Radom workers. By this stage, the authorities had begun to deploy a policy of seeking to isolate the WDC from the workers, notably by organising petitions against the WDC. The response from among the workers was poor.

18 Jan. *Trybuna Ludu* hinted that the WDC had been guilty of spreading false information in persisting with its allegations against the police and noted that 58 people were still in prison.

20 Jan. The WDC stated that it would defy official attempts to se-questrate its funds, standing at around 2 million zlotys, through court action.

22 Jan. Andrzejewski and another WDC member Halina Mikołajska summoned to appear before People's Court on charges of illegal fund raising, but refused to do so. They were fined 5000 zlotys each.

24 Jan. The Polish Ministry of Religious Affairs issued a decree cut-ting off funds from the independent Club of Catholic Intellectuals (KIK).

29 Jan. A new series of letters sent to the Sejm protesting against alleged police brutality during the June events. Among the signatories there were 61 priest, 13 sociologists and 31 "sympathisers of the WDC".

1 Feb. 22 members of the WDC signed a brief message of solidarity with human rights campaigners in Czechoslovakia, adding their voices to Soviet dissident Andrei Sakharov and 30 Hungarian intellectuals.

3 Feb. Addressing workers in the tractor factory in Ursus — the very place where disturbances started on 25 June 1976, Mr. Gierek said he planned to announce an amnesty for imprisoned workers who regret their part in the June food price riots. He then attacked the intellectuals who had been helping the workers (353 workers were tried on various charges; most of them had their sentences commuted, but about 33 are still in goal).

5 Feb. The WDC responded by stating at a press conference that it will not dissolve itself until a total and unconditional amnesty is granted and until the workers released from prison are reinstated in their jobs at their former salaries.

9 Feb. 157th Episcopal Conference meets, approves Memorandum on Population Policies, prepares programme for renewal of Vows of Jasnogóra.

16 Feb. WDC's communiqué, membership 23: press release of 5 Feb. repeated; Radom: 12 workers released, 2 reinstated at work; Ursus workers reportedly encouraged to apply for reinstatement providing they fill-in official forms of repentance; internal party circular leaked, quoting 634 arrests in Radom, 172 in Ursus, 55 in Płock, of these 334 tried by tribunals, 52 in accelerated court proceedings; same source claims 27 out of 60 questioned reaffirmed complaints of police violence but "investigations left no grounds to believe that agents had applied force": apart from 4 verified cases of death in Radom evidence of others conflicting: 965 cases of reprisals investigated, 493 assisted, over 2 millions zlotys disbursed. Petition for Parliamentary Inquiry: 965 signatories.

23 Feb. At a press conference in Warsaw Gierek said petitions "cannot be disregarded or under-estimated but should not be over-estimated". Episcopate are "reasonable".

24 Feb. PAP, the official press agency, publishes Episcopate's statement warning of a falsified edition of a book of Cardinal Wyszyński's sermons.

9 March. Petition for Parliamentary Inquiry signed by 730 Warsaw students, delivered by delegation of 10.

10 March. WDC calls attention to a new wave of police violence and harassment in Radom "recalling the worst times of the Stalinist era".

16 March. Böll, Kołakowski, Michnik give press conference in Cologne appealing to governments and public opinion to pressurize E. European governments to respect human and civil rights; they send (on 17th) telegram of sympathy at Prof. Patocka's death.

22 March. Petition by 517 Cracow students delivered to Parliament by writer Brandys. Similar petition by 285 students of the Catholic University of Lublin.

23 March. Barańczak arrested in Cracow for alleged breaking of exchange control regulations; wife of Brożyna arrested in Radom for alleged murder of husband.

25 March. *Deutsche National Zeitung* published article supposedly by Michnik and Kołakowski, a secret-police forgery implicating authors in links with W. German revanchism.

27 March. Movement for Human and Civil Rights founded "to inform the public and the pertinent authorities of all violations of human and civil rights and to bring assistance where possible".

29 March. WDC condemns the Rector of Warsaw University for threatening disciplinary action against the 730 student-petitioners.

29 March. Majewski's and Żukowski's sentences of 3 years upheld.

5 April. WDC press conference draws attention to "increased activity of security organs aimed at withdrawing relaxations"; police cover-up of Brożyna's murder disclosed.

11 April. Czesław Chomicki, serving 6 year sentence, stages new series of hunger strikes in a bid for justice. WDC appeals for clemency and calls for speedier application of amnesty to over 20 prisoners still remaining.

14 April. Plenary meeting of Polish Party Central Committee. Gierek promises "all necessary means" will be used against enemies of the communist system, a forecast of stronger reprisals against WDC.

14, 15, 16 April. Kuroń, Chojecki, Macierewicz and other collaborators arrested and held for 48 hours.

15 April. Movement for Human and Civil Rights issues statement calling for immediate release of 20 prisoners still held and reinstatement of those dismissed from work in the June events.

21 April Kuroń informs Reuter that 10 Radom prisoners were released.

23 April. Kuroń, Chojecki, Naimski, Macierewicz arrested and held for 48 hours.

24 April. Pastoral Letter decries discrimination against believers and the plague of alcoholism.

29 April. Kuroń and Lipski questioned under Art. 132 (contacts with foreign anti-Polish agencies).

3 May. WDC press conference: Michnik joins as 24th member. Renewal of Vows of Jasnogóra: Card. Wyszyński's sermon states that "it is not enough to request ... we have also the duty to demand"; Michnik questioned under Art. 132.

4 May. 158th Episcopal Conference calls to attention the inhumane conditions of work in the mines.

7 May. Stanisław Pyjas, student collaborator of WDC, found dead in Cracow.

9 May. WDC calls for public investigation into circumstances of Pyjas' death: reveals that Pyjas and others received anonymous threat notes.

10 May. WDC informs of ever more frequent violations of legality; dismissal of its members and collaborators. WDC forms a Standing Bureau for Interventions to gather information on violations of human and civil rights and to bring aid where possible.

15 May. Pyjas' funeral marked by peaceful, silent march of 5000 through Cracow. Students form a "Committee for Student Solidarity" "the Socialist Students' Union has lost the ultimate moral right to represent the academic community". Kuroń and others arrested and so prevented from attending.

16 May. Janiurek, Government spokesman, claims that the Cracow demonstration was "provoked" by WDC.

17 May. CSS declare themselves ready to help victims of repression; WDC demands immediate release of Kuroń, Macierewicz, Michnik, Naimski, Ostrowski, who are now held under the "procurator's sanction" since the 48-hour arrest has elapsed.

18 May. 17 writers appeal for release. "We know them not to be criminals but very devoted community workers."

19 May. Lipski also arrested.

25 May. Hunger strikes staged simultaneously by Chomicki in Radom, and in solidarity by the WDC prisoners in Warsaw, also by a group of WDC supporters and co-workers, 14 in all, at the Church of St. Martin, Warsaw.

1 June. *The Times* reports Russian dissidents' solidarity with WDC.
9 June. Reuter reports that Lipski released. PEN Club had appealed on his behalf in late May.
10 June. Corpus Christi. In his sermon Cardinal Wyszyński warns against further violations of human and civil rights.
22 July. WDC members and collaborators released. All the workers arrested as a result of the June events now free.